FOOD LOVERS'
GUIDE TO
NORTH CAROLINA'S
OUTER BANKS

Help Us Keep This Guide Up to Date

We would love to hear from you concerning your experiences with this guide and how you feel it could be improved and kept up to date. Please send your comments and suggestions to:

editorial@GlobePequot.com

Thanks for your input, and happy travels!

FOOD LOVERS' SERIES

FOOD LOVERS'
GUIDE TO
NORTH CAROLINA'S
OUTER BANKS

The Best Restaurants, Markets & Local Culinary Offerings

1st Edition

Elizabeth Wiegand

Guilford, Connecticut

Editor: Amy Lyons
Project Editor: Lynn Zelem
Layout Artist: Mary Ballachino
Text Design: Sheryl Kober
Illustrations by Jill Butler with additional art by Carleen Moira Powell and MaryAnn Dubé
Maps: Alena Joy Pearce © Morris Book Publishing, LLC

ISSN 2327-9427
ISBN 978-0-7627-8113-3

Printed in the United States of America
10 9 8 7 6 5 4 3 2 1

All the information in this guidebook is subject to change. We recommend that you call ahead to obtain current information before traveling.

For my willing and adventurous eating life partner
and terrific father of our three lovely daughters, Steven Wiegand

Contents

Recipes, 181

Appendices, 211

About the Author

Behind every good bite of food, there's a good story, says Elizabeth Wiegand, a self-described "foodie" from back when the term was first used. Wherever she has traveled, she's not only tasted but also gotten the culinary history of each dish. She's eaten her way up and down the coast of North Carolina, across the state, and through the Blue Ridge Mountains. With travels in Europe, the Caribbean, Central America, and the South Pacific, whether sailing or diving or driving, she's found great foods and the stories behind them.

Elizabeth grew up landlocked, on a tobacco farm in central NC that has been in her family since the 1840s, and learned to garden and cook under her grandmother's tutelage. On her honeymoon, she spent the whole summer at NC's coast, fishing and cooking the daily catch with her husband, Steve. She was hooked for lifetime trips to the beach from then on. Elizabeth and Steve raised three daughters, many dogs, and even a parrot. They currently reside in Raleigh, where they can reach either the mountains or the coast within hours.

Elizabeth is the author of *The Outer Banks Cookbook: Recipes & Traditions from North Carolina's Barrier Islands,* Second Edition, and *The New Blue Ridge Cookbook: Authentic Recipes from Virginia Highlands to NC Mountains,* both by Globe Pequot Press. You can follow her eating and travel stories at Carolinafoodie.blogspot.com.

Acknowledgments

When you grow up on a farm, you quickly learn about the circle of life—how the seeds you plant grow into the veggies to be harvested, then cooked, and placed on the dinner plate before you; how the milk you coax from the old broad can be made into the ice cream you adore; or how the calf you've raised becomes the steak on your plate. I am grateful to my family and my farm background in the fertile soil near Stem, North Carolina, for that has helped me see that with hard work and a lot of respect and appreciation for the gifts of nature, the world can be my oyster.

This farm background also helps me to appreciate the hard work that others do to bring food to my table. Like the fishermen who leave before first light to set nets or pull pots in the cold dawn, returning only when the sun is getting ready to set. Then it's to market, where they hope to make enough money to cover the fuel and boat costs. The journey from their boat to my plate takes a lot of sweat yet a love for this way of life. I admire that.

When I fell in love, with a man who would become my partner in life and with the ocean he introduced me to, I discovered a world of seafood beyond the fried variety I'd previously encountered. Our shared love for the beach, for catching blues or crabs, or digging clams, for stuffing our ice chest with shrimp and crabmeat at the market, has led to many, many soul-satisfying trips to the North

Carolina coast and a lifetime of good eating. I am so grateful for that privilege and thankful to Steve for sharing.

Much love and many thanks go to my good friend Della Basnight, a Manteo native and proud Outer Banker. She opened her own doors and heart, and convinced many locals who didn't know this nosy writer from Raleigh to do the same. We've shared and critiqued many meals together and she's told many stories about life in the Outer Banks. Also many thanks to Vicki Basnight, who shared her wisdom about wines to pair with seafood, and who took me out with her team to pull crab pots, opening my eyes to what hard work that is. To Lynne Foster, who invited me to be a part of the Days at the Docks festival in Hatteras, because that enlightened me about the issues that commercial fishermen face today to keep their business viable.

And I'd especially like to thank the many chefs, restaurateurs, fishermen, and market folks in the Outer Banks who opened their kitchens and coolers to share their passionate visions of what good, local seafood is all about. These are the real foodies and the ones who make all that good eating happen.

Finally, I send many thanks to Amy Lyons and Lynn Zelem, editors at Globe Pequot Press, who take my words and polish them up. Y'all do a good job of trying to understand the idioms and phrases of this Southerner.

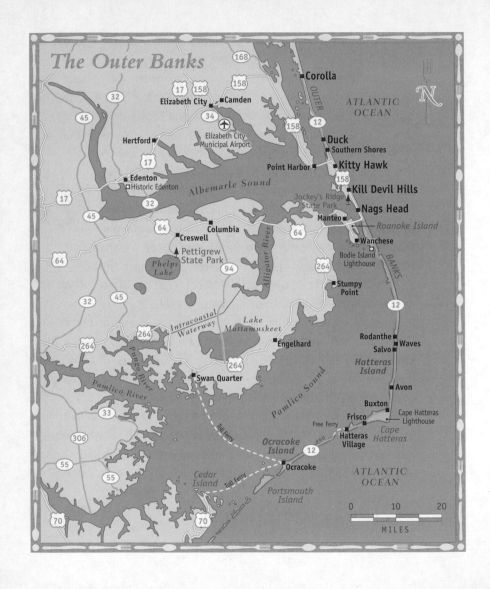

Introduction

Some folks flock to the Outer Banks to catch some rays and laze in the sand. Others come to catch the big, rolling surf as storms approach, while others catch the wind that propels them on boards or kites in the shallow waters of the sound. Still others climb the highest sand dune on the East Coast to catch the famed wind of the Wright Brothers and soar with a hang glider.

Fishermen come in droves as big as the schools of fish they hope to catch, dreaming of trophies to hang on the wall or to cook on the grill. They stand for hours in the icy surf, casting again and again and sometimes striking lucky with running schools of stripers or drums. Or they'll endure bumpy boat rides out on the water to the Yellow Brick Road, what locals call the Gulf Stream, to jig for the groupers or wahoo that hang out at those reefs. When they get back to the harbor, they pose with big fat grins and their (hopefully) big catch.

Not me. I just come to the Outer Banks to catch a bite to eat.

As a self-proclaimed foodie for more years than I'd care to admit, I have eaten my way from where the road ends in Corolla all the way down to where NC 12 Highway ends at the ferry dock in Ocracoke.

Give me a dish of just-warmed jumbo lump crabmeat panned in butter and I feel that I've died and gone to heaven. Grill me some soft-shells and douse them with a bit of spicy remoulade, and hey, that's so fine. Fry me up some hush puppies and shrimp, and I'll gladly wipe the grease from my chin. I've spent many a happy hour at the table with loved ones, drinking a cold brew and peeling shrimp or cracking crabs. And I've warmed my happy taste buds with a hot, slippery oyster from Rose Bay, just steamed or grilled open and dunked in melted butter.

My sojourns up and down these long stretches of white, sandy beaches have landed me in some mighty fine restaurants, where I learned to love the Hatteras-style chowder that's full of clams but no dairy. I've had daily doses of mahimahi, or what locals call dolphinfish, panfried and grilled. And yellowfin tuna, so fresh you could swear it was still wiggling, seared yet with a bright pink interior, served with pickled ginger and wasabi. I couldn't tell you which is better—shrimp panned in butter, marinated and then grilled, or slightly battered, then fried. And I learned where to find crab cakes made with little or no filler.

I eat well on the Outer Banks, don't you think? You can, too.

Buy Local, Fresh from the Boat to Your Table

Harvesting food from the water has always been a way of life on the Outer Banks. Since the 1700s, commercial fishermen have kept tables full and coastal economies thriving.

However, commercial fishing has been affected this last decade by environmental factors and increases in regulations and fuel costs. Sustainability and overfishing have been issues with some catches.

But the biggest challenge to the thousand fishermen from Wanchese, Ocracoke, and other Outer Banks fishing communities is imported seafood. Here's a frightening statistic: 90 percent of all seafood served nationally is imported. Only 2 percent of that imported seafood faces inspection by the US Food and Drug Administration. Imports also drive down earnings for US fishermen, and at times compromise the quality of both the environment and seafood.

To resist these problems, Outer Banks fishermen, some of them multigenerational watermen, are working together with local seafood markets and grocers, and local restaurants, thanks to grants by the **Golden LEAF Foundation.** Their mission? To help preserve their fishing heritage and bring healthy and sustainable seafood to the table that's from local waters.

Customers should look for the logo of a plate encircled with OUTER BANKS CATCH to find restaurants and seafood markets that offer locally caught seafood (outerbankscatch.com). They should also look for the OCRACOKE FRESH logo when they are on Ocracoke Island. It identifies local, hand-caught seafood brought fresh from the boat (ocracokeseafood.com).

Why Being a Locavore Matters

My favorite restaurants are run by chefs who insist on sourcing their seafood and fresh produce locally. And that's not easy. That means their menus change with every season, for some fish migrate, crabs winter in the mud, and shrimp hide in the marsh grass. You have to understand that you just can't have what you want exactly when you want it if you're going to "go local" and support the struggling commercial fishermen of the Outer Banks. It would be much easier for chefs to just order foods from the cheapest sources that come from all over the place.

When you buy local, you're supporting the person who spends grueling hours on the water to bring your seafood dinner to your table. You're also supporting the markets and gal behind the counter who sell you that fish or shrimp. And you're putting not only local chefs but waitstaff, busboys, and dishwashers to work. And accountants, lawyers, truck drivers, and others involved in running local businesses like restaurants and markets.

That's why you'll find I've noted if a restaurant serves local seafood especially. It's important, y'all. You, too, as a consumer can insist or recommend that your favorite eating places make the effort to source ingredients from local farmers, producers, and watermen.

Note: Stormy Weather

Hurricanes have historically wreaked havoc on the Outer Banks, because it sticks so far out into the Atlantic on the Southeast coast. Most recently, Hurricane Irene hit in 2011, and flooded much of the Outer Banks, particularly Manteo and on the soundside of the strip from Kitty Hawk to Nags Head, destroying homes and businesses. On Hatteras Island, NC 12 Highway is the paved artery to the mainland, and it was destroyed in several places. A new inlet was created, and a temporary bridge was finally installed to allow traffic to flow again. Homes, markets, and restaurants like Mack Daddy's in Avon were so flooded they were closed for months.

A year later, in 2012, Sandy hit the North Carolina coast before traveling north to devastate New Jersey and New York shores. Huge surf and winds in Kitty Hawk from Hurricane Sandy flattened the dunes protecting the Beach Road and flooded homes and businesses all the way to the Bypass. On Hatteras Island, dunes protecting NC 12 were again flattened, and waves crashed over the roadway and knocked down homes. NC 12 was closed to all but four-wheel-drive vehicles for months, isolating many Hatteras residents.

As of this writing, the Bonner Bridge over Oregon Inlet is to be replaced, NC 12 on Hatteras Island continues to need clearing after storms, and the ferry from Hatteras to Ocracoke often encounters delays caused by shoaling in the Pamlico Sound. But traffic eventually flows, thanks to diligent work crews.

Residents of the Outer Banks are a sturdy, optimistic bunch. They're survivalists, and accept that this gorgeous place they call home, which most times provides a bounty of nature to enjoy, can be a difficult place to live. Storms may knock them around, but they'll make it back. And so do visitors. Once you've gotten a taste of the Outer Banks, you'll want to return again and again.

How to Use This Book

As a food lovers' guide, this book has broken the Outer Banks into geographical segments, starting with Corolla and heading down the beach all the way to Ocracoke. Each segment features a list of food stuff you don't want to miss.

It is noted when each restaurant or market provides you with local foods. And throughout, you'll also find sidebars offering tips on buying seafood or "insider" information about local foods. There are also descriptions of the few breweries and wineries in or near the Outer Banks.

A variety of restaurants await you in the Outer Banks. Almost every single one listed here focuses on the best of what's available, and that's fresh seafood. You'll find a range of price points, from inexpensive family places and local hangouts, like Sam & Omie's, to pricier, elegant dining rooms like Manteo's 1587. Some, like Owens', have been in business with the same family running it for decades. And I've made a point of omitting any chain restaurants or franchises, because there are too many good, independent places that are unique to the Outer Banks. Most are informal, where you can wear shorts and flip-flops, but a few expect your best attire.

And please note that each restaurant included has its own atmosphere, attitude, ambience, and signature dishes that I've tried to convey to you. My descriptions are just that, not reviews. That said, if I really like a place, you'll know!

Weather, the economy, and other factors affect businesses, and many may change or close. Give them a call or look them up before you go.

Foodie Faves

The restaurants that have made this section are the most noteworthy establishments that are worth a visit, from long-standing favorites to the latest on the scene. Bon appétit!

Specialty Stores, Markets & Fishmongers

Some truly notable fish shops, specialized groceries, farmers' markets, etc., can be found along the Outer Banks. Here we give you a list of the top specialty stores.

Recipes

At the back of the book (p. 181) we give new meaning to the phrase "continuing education" and help you re-create some of our favorite local dishes.

Price Code

Whether you want an inexpensive fish taco or shrimp burger, or feel like a splurge with a lovely multicourse dinner with nice wine, you'll find a choice of restaurants in every region of the Outer Banks to meet your desires. Each restaurant listing under Foodie Faves includes the following price code that will give you an idea of what the price of an entree may be.

$	less than $10
$$	$10 to $20
$$$	$20 to $30
$$$$	$30 to $40

Getting Around the Outer Banks

Bridges and ferries are required to enter the Outer Banks, the string of barrier islands linked to a long, skinny fingerlike peninsula that extends from the Virginia border via the beach.

Visitors from the north will most likely arrive via US Highway 158, from the section of Currituck County on the mainland, crossing over to the area at the northern end of Kitty Hawk on the Wright Memorial Bridge. At the junction with NC 12 Highway, visitors can head north to Southern Shores, Duck, and finally to Corolla, where the highway ends and travelers must hope for low tide to drive on the beach, with no pavement, up to Carova and the Virginia border.

As you continue south on US Highway 158, this five-lane roadway is referred to by the locals as the Bypass. Officially, it's Croatan Highway. Kitty Hawk and then Kill Devil Hills are noted with a North Croatan Highway address.

Continue south on the Bypass and you'll hit Nags Head, which has a South Croatan address. Keep going further south to Whalebone Junction, where US 64/264 crosses over the Causeway from Roanoke Island, home to Manteo and Wanchese. (Note that US 64 makes a 600-mile run from Manteo to Murphy, NC, in the mountains at the Tennessee border.)

Road Rules

Along this stretch of beach communities, there's a milepost designation used by businesses and restaurants to help visitors find them, with a green sign posted every half mile. These are designated as

MP in this book. The Outer Banks Visitor Center marks the beginning at MP 1, as everyone refers to it, and continues south to Nags Head and Whalebone Junction, which is at MP 16. Even on Hatteras Island, some businesses refer to their mileposts, too, which are up in the 70s.

Now, to confuse you further, there's also another main drag that runs along these beach communities. It's called the Beach Road by the locals, but is formally named Virginia Dare Trail. Locals say "up the beach" when they mean northern communities, or "down the beach." Corresponding milepost signs are also used.

Local Outer Bankers also talk about going "down Hatteras." To get to Hatteras Island, at Whalebone Junction, go due south on NC 12 Highway, the only paved option to get down the beach. You'll enter the Cape Hatteras National Seashore, which stretches over 75 miles of gorgeous, white-sand beaches and sand dunes, undeveloped in most areas. You'll first encounter the Pea Island National Wildlife Refuge, where literally hundreds of thousands of tundra swans, Canadian geese, and other birds flock each winter.

Cross over the Bonner Bridge that straddles Oregon Inlet. The villages of Hatteras Island all stretch on either side of NC 12 Highway between the beach and the sound-side, where settlers originally built their homes. I love the village names—Rodanthe, Waves, Salvo, Avon, Buxton, Frisco, and finally at the tip, Hatteras Village.

Catch the ferry from Hatteras to cross the Pamlico Sound and Hatteras Inlet to Ocracoke Island. You can take this ferry for free, whether by car, bicycle, or as a passenger. After the ferry lands, there's nothing but NC 12 Highway, with the beach on the left and the marsh and sound on the right, for 13 long and lovely miles. You'll pass a campground and pony pen, where the famed Outer Banks wild horses are kept safe from running into vehicles.

Ocracoke Village is at the end of NC 12 Highway, which here is known as the Irvin Garrish Highway. It winds along the waterfront of Silver Lake harbor, and ends at the ferry terminal where you can go to the mainland via toll ferries to Cedar Island or Swan Quarter.

And, all up and down this vast area of absolutely gorgeous beaches, there are great places to find the freshest of seafood. Stop and eat!

Food Festivals & Events

Check out these special foodie events that occur annually on the Outer Banks that are sure to delight your palate:

March

Taste of the Beach, obxtasteofthebeach.com. Held over a 4-day weekend in mid-March, usually during St. Patrick's Day weekend, this annual foodie event is one that you don't want to miss. It's not just special dinners or wine tastings, but also tapas and pub crawls, restaurant tours to meet the chefs and owners and taste inside their kitchens, and more, like the 2012 ceviche and tequila tasting and another featuring coffee cuppings, all spread out in venues up and down the beaches. The culminating event is the Grand Tasting, with about 20 restaurants along with beverage vendors presenting samples at one venue to compete for the Best in Show and People's Choice awards. Events sell out quickly, so get on their e-mail list or become a Facebook friend.

June

Knotts Island Peach Festival, knottsislandonline.com. Take a ferry ride over to this festival of all things "peachy," as in fresh peaches, peach pies, and peach ice cream. You'll also see a parade, a lawnmower racing show, live music, crafts, games, and rides for the kids. Held the third weekend in June at the Ruritan Community Park, its proceeds benefit community projects.

September

Day at the Docks, Hatteras Docks, dayatthedocks.org. Held the third Saturday in September, the Day at the Docks festival got its start because of Hurricane Isabel, which devastated the roads, homes, and businesses of Hatteras Island in 2003. To celebrate the coming together of the community and the efforts that commercial and charter fishermen made to help all recover and survive, organizers put together what has become an annual event to honor the heritage and living traditions of Hatteras watermen. Fishing and net demos by working watermen, a chowder competition, oral histories, games, live music, children's crab races and fishing contests, local seafood to taste, and a Chef's Throwdown are held, now over a period of several days. The sweetest and most memorable to me was watching the parade of boats gliding by for the Blessing of the Fleet. Unfortunately a series of hurricanes, Irene and Sandy especially, and a few nor'easters in the last few years have wreaked havoc with Hatteras Island, which only adds additional significance to Day at the Docks. This is an event on the Outer Banks that you should not miss.

Currituck Fall Food & Wine Festival, sanctuaryvineyards.com. Live music, Great Currituck Grape Stomp, Pork and Cork BBQ competition, local wines and beers, and local food vendors featuring the cuisine from the waters and fields of Currituck County. Held at The Cotton Gin in Jarvisburg the fourth Saturday in September.

October

The Outer Banks Seafood Festival, outerbanksseafoodfestival .org, at the Old Windmill Point in Nags Head. See the boats that are used to bring seafood to your table, like the flat boats used to haul in crab pots, or replicas of a 19th-century shad boat and a sharpie.

You can also watch hands-on demonstrations by working watermen and cooking demonstrations, participate in cook-offs, and taste samples from local seafood restaurants. Information about marine ecology and sea life, and traditions of this coastal community can be found in the educational tent. Vendors offer coastal crafts. Held the third Saturday in October.

October/November

Fall Restaurant Week, outerbanksrestaurantweek.com. Sponsored by the Outer Banks Restaurant Association, this event showcases local fare and promotes the Outer Banks as a dining destination. Participating restaurants feature their own special prix-fixe, three-course menus at a reasonable set price. (A similar week is held each spring.) Plus, Restaurant Week culminates in the **Outer Banks Chili Cookoff,** a people's choice contest among participating restaurants for the best beef, non-beef, vegetarian, and overall best chili. It's a family-friendly event, with live music and beer and wine for sale. Held from the end of October to early November.

The Signature Chefs Auction, Outer Banks, hrsigchef.com/outer-banks/index.html. For this charity event for the March of Dimes, several Outer Banks chefs present tasting samples during a reception, as well as donate unique dining packages that attendees can bid on. It's a lovely way to combine good, local food and nice wines to benefit a very worthwhile cause. Held in late fall or winter.

December

Oyster Roast & Steam Shrimp Fund-raiser, at the Fish House in Ocracoke, ocracokewatermen.org. Ocracoke Working Watermen's Association holds this delicious event every year at the last remaining fish house on the waterfront of Silver Lake, which they helped save a few years ago. A fish stew from one of the island's oldest families, the O'Neals, is also available. After the roast, drop by the OWWA's exhibit in the small boathouse nearby for dessert and hot cider around the wood stove. Held the last weekend in December.

The Cuisine of the Outer Banks

Mention the Outer Banks and some foodies think of soft-shells. Or stewed blue crabs. Or maybe they conjure up stripers, what some call rockfish or even Mr. Pajama Pants (for their striped sides!). The cuisine of the Outer Banks you'll find today is varied, including traditional dishes, globally influenced contemporary dishes using local foods, and produce from just across the sounds on the mainland. Seasons affect what's available at markets, as they do in any region of the world.

Here are some tips about what kinds of foods to expect at Outer Banks eateries and markets.

Seafood Is Seasonal

Menus on the Outer Banks typically feature a daily special that highlights a fresh, local catch. Like fruits and veggies, most fish and shellfish are seasonal, so they migrate to the waters of the

Outer Banks or are at the stage of perfection only during either cold or warm weather, although there are a few fish that hang around all year.

Cold-Weather Seafoods include flounder (locals may call them "flukes"), bluefish, croaker, king mackerel, sea bass, grey sea trout, spotted sea trout, striped bass (rockfish), spot, and oysters.

Warm-Weather Seafoods are shrimp, blue crabs, soft-shell crabs (mid-spring), mahimahi, Spanish mackerel, tilefish, and mullet.

Year-Round Seafoods are clams, tuna, grouper, snapper, and triggerfish.

Outer Banks Traditions from the Sea

Yes, we're aware that further north, as in Maryland, they claim blue crabs as their own. But so do the Outer Banks. And our green-tail shrimp are the best! And soft-shells? Colington Island is their capital, right? Here are some of the tasty components of coastal cuisine that the Outer Banks are mighty proud of.

Eat Shrimp? Naw, They're Bugs!

Shrimping is the largest seafood industry in North Carolina. Today, dozens of shrimp boats leave the Wanchese harbor, their wings of nets ready to be lowered into the waters of Pamlico Sound or just offshore.

But old-timers in the Outer Banks did not eat shrimp. It wasn't until the 1930s that folks in the Outer Banks started placing what they considered a pest that fouled up their nets into the frying pan.

"My grandmother thought they were worms," said Della Basnight, a Manteo native. "She wouldn't eat them. Thought we were crazy. They were bugs, for God's sake."

My 97-year-old buddy, John Gaskill, reported seeing them in the ocean grass while he was out fishing, but when he left Wanchese for the Navy in 1933, "we weren't eating shrimp. We thought they were bugs."

Settlers in New Orleans and the Louisiana bayou country were hauling in shrimp for dining tables early in the 1700s. That culinary tradition inched its way up through the coastal area of Georgia to South Carolina's Low Country, where shrimp and grits became a favorite breakfast dish.

As diesel engines were adapted for boats, netting shrimp became easier. Southport, near Wilmington and the SC border, was the first seaport in NC to build a shrimp cannery in the early 1900s. Several Wanchese fishermen headed to the Gulf of Mexico during the 1930s to learn how to trawl for shrimp, and returned to establish a slowly profitable industry. Ice plants, like the one on "Ice Plant Island" on Roanoke Island that's now the Roanoke Island Festival Park, helped preserve their catch.

Early shrimpers were called "bug hunters" along the coast of North Carolina. As eating shrimp caught on, the statewide haul grew. Today, more than 10 million pounds are caught in the wild each year.

Outer Banks Catch & Ocracoke Fresh

For generations, fishermen have made a living supplying our tables with great tasting seafood from the waters surrounding the Outer Banks. But it's a way of life that's struggling to keep afloat, mainly due to imported seafood, increased regulations, and rising costs.

To fight against this tide, fishermen have joined forces with local seafood markets and restaurants, thanks to grants by the Golden LEAF Foundation. The goals of this joint venture, the Outer Banks Catch program, are to help preserve the fishing heritage of commercial fishing families, to bring healthy and sustainable seafood to the table, and to make it easy for the consumer to tell which businesses support local fishermen.

Look for the logo OUTER BANKS CATCH to find restaurants and seafood markets that offer mostly local, not imported, seafood. Visit outerbankscatch.com.

On Ocracoke Island, the Ocracoke Working Watermen's Association adopted the logo OCRACOKE FRESH, to let consumers know which establishments use local, hand-caught seafood fresh from the boat. Visit ocracokeseafood.com.

Green Tails

You might see or hear, during the late summer or early fall, an excited proclamation that the green tails are here! And no, it's not a scourge or something to worry about like Paul Revere's Redcoats.

Green tails are officially known as white shrimp, and are one of the three types of shrimp that swim in the waters of the Outer

Banks. Since they have the most delicate flavor, they're the ones most prized by chefs and shrimp connoisseurs. Although cooking shrimp with their heads and/or shells gives most dishes more flavor, it's more convenient to have them already cleaned when freezing for use in the winter. So like many chefs on the Outer Banks, I find a source and stash dozens of pounds of green tails in one-dish packets in my freezer.

And the other types of shrimp? Brown shrimp are the most prevalent during the summer, and they're what you'll find at the seafood markets. Large pink or spotted shrimp are harvested more in the cooler waters of spring or fall. And lately, shrimpers have hauled in a few specimens of huge tiger shrimp, an import and a menace to our species.

A shrimp's life is very transient. They're spawned in the ocean, then carried by tides and wind-driven currents into the sounds and estuaries where they overwinter. Fast growers, they double in size every two weeks! Brown shrimp mature within 18 months. So when they're almost fully grown, like our teenagers they're anxious to leave their nesting waters for the big wide ocean.

Oysters

Oysters were nearly wiped out from North Carolina's waters during the last few decades due to the usual reasons: overharvesting and habitat disturbances, and a nasty little parasite called dermo. So the state worked to clean up the water, limit catches and coastal development, and maintain a number of oyster sanctuaries along the coast. Although there is still some concern for oysters, commercial landings have been up.

Rose Bay and other shallow bays close to the mainland near Lake Mattamuskeet and Swan Quarter on the Pamlico Sound are the source for many of the oysters that show up on Outer Banks menus. Mounds of oyster shells remain at many local Native American haunts, like at the Great Gut out of Wanchese.

Just a short skiff's ride from Hatteras Island, a special new reef has attracted attention and oysters. Built by sixth, seventh, and eighth graders at Cape Hatteras Secondary School of Coastal Studies at Buxton, it is a collaborative project between the school, the UNC Coastal Studies Institute, the Nature Conservancy, and the state's innovative recycling program.

These middle school students take weekend and holiday time to bag recycled oyster shells, then haul them out in a skiff to a reef where they are placed to attract oyster larvae. Students snorkel on the reef during the school year to count growth and witness other fish hanging around their reef. And, they look forward to harvesting those new oysters within 3 years.

To recycle your own oyster shells, check this website for recycling centers: ncfisheries.net/shellfish/recyle5.htm.

Yellowfin Tuna

Yellowfin tuna show up along the Outer Banks at what I consider the prettiest times of the year, both spring and fall.

Best bets for fresh sushi or slightly seared tuna are during cool days, when the sun casts a longer shadow, particularly mid-September through the end of November. That's when these yellow canaries of the water begin to school on the edge of the Gulf Stream as it almost licks Cape Hatteras on its way north. But like the snow-birds in the Inland Waterway during the fall, the tuna are headed south, to warmer waters.

And like tourists further south, yellowfins like to swim with the dolphins, feeding on squid and fast fish. Built like a torpedo, tuna are lightning-fast swimmers, some of the quickest in the ocean.

That's what makes them an exciting catch, and what also makes their muscles, the loins, such a great steak on your plate. Outer Banks

CATCHING SOFT-SHELL CRABS

How the soft-shell crab makes it to our tables is a fascinating story.

Jimmies, or males, spend the winter buried in the mucky mud of estuaries, while sallies prefer deeper sandy bottoms in the sounds. When the water begins to warm, they emerge from their hibernation, looking for what else but food, and, well, sex.

It seems the sallies that are ready to become sexually mature (when they'll become sooks) awaken rather randy. They're the ones that didn't get to do "it" before their long winter's sleep, for most scientists believe that females get to mate only once in their life, and then they die. During this spring ritual, they're truly driven, and can actually sniff out a good mate, for males emit a pheromone when they're ready.

So they all head to the bar scene, well, actually shallow waters where they cruise the appetizers and available mates. Then, it's the males who go all out to attract attention, performing a kind of Steve Martin Crazy Guy Macarena dance, waving claws and kicking up sand. She coolly claps. Then he taps her claws, and if she's really interested, she tucks her claws in and allows him to carry her off with his walking legs.

He will "cradle carry" her for a couple of days while she readies to shed, protecting her from predators. Then he stands guard while she "undresses," for which he's rewarded as she experiences mating for the only time in her life. Tuckered out and weak-kneed, she's cradled once again, protected by her lover.

She'll then instinctively make her way to the estuaries. Mass migrations of sooks have been witnessed, and it's what crabbers wait for. She'll eventually develop eggs and spawn at least once or twice (his sperm lasts for maybe a year), and perhaps overwinter and spawn again the following season, before she dies. Crabs caught with an orange egg sac are called sponge crabs, and should be returned to the water.

Meanwhile, jimmy just hangs out and finds other sallies and sooks to woo, protect, and mate with.

That's the logic behind a "jimmy pot," one way to catch a bunch of "peelers" in season. It's a little like operating a bordello, with genders reversed.

Mike Cox, who worked at Jughead Etheridge's shedder on Manteo's Shallowbag Bay, explained it to me several years ago. "To catch a female, you put a jimmy in the bait pocket, 'cause she's seeking him out when she's ready to mate. So when she comes in, he carries her on upstairs. That's when we call her a 'chandler's wife,' and she'll shed."

But a "peeler pot" works even better. A jimmy is placed in a special holding cell, so no female can actually get to him. His pheromone may attract up to 20 or so females, all ready to shed. Bingo for the crabber!

Crabs ready to molt, or shed, are then sold to "shedders," who operate holding tanks kept at the right temperature and who pluck the crabs as soon as they shed.

restaurants not only slice these tuna into sushi, but blacken, sear, or grill them, serving them with wasabi or perhaps a seaweed salad.

Blue Crabs

Callinectes sapidus, the scientific name for the blue crab found in North Carolina, means "beautiful swimmers." One bite of the luscious, steamed meat from a Beautiful Swimmer can send me floating into ecstasy. Crabmeat is my absolute favorite thing to eat, and it is so easy to prepare.

Most of NC's blue crabs are found in the Albemarle and Pamlico Sounds, so you'll find more crab processors in Manteo and Wanchese, then further south and up the Neuse River at Oriental and New Bern. Most seafood markets will have cooked, picked crabmeat for sale in 1-pound plastic tubs.

Crabmeat is sold as jumbo or lump, which comes from the prime lumps of meat found under the shell; backfin, a lower grade that includes some lumps; and the claw meat, which has a more intense flavor. Look for containers of claw meat still attached to the last claw joint, which are great appetizers for dipping into cocktail sauce.

There's nothing finer than a pound of jumbo lump crabmeat, for which you'll spend a pretty penny, but it's worth it. Do as little as possible to it. Sautéed in a little butter, dusted with Old Bay seasoning and maybe add a little chopped chive, and you've got a divine dish.

Soft-Shell Crabs

Come the first full moon in May, get ready for soft-shell crabs. That's when lovers of this succulent treat, like me, can't wait to devour the whole thing—claws, legs and all.

Nearly nude, caught while its protective layer is being retailored, a soft-shell is one of the best delicacies ever retrieved from the estuaries and sounds of the Outer Banks.

No matter how they're "fixed," soft-shells offer up the sweetest, most delectable flavor. I've died and gone to heaven eating sautéed or gently fried soft-shells at Basnight's Lone Cedar on the causeway near Nags Head. Fried soft-shells stuffed in a bun with coleslaw, found at many Outer Banks eateries, rival any lobster roll. Dajio's in Ocracoke serves soft-shells tempura-style with a sassy salsa. And I've loved them gussied up with peanuts, country ham, and green onions at The Blue Point in Duck. At home, we just simply grill them with lemon, butter, and a bit of hot sauce.

Crabs live in tune with the moon, peeling off their skins and mating according to lunar phases. Before they mature, they pass through 20 or more molts. Spring is the prime season for soft-shells, from mid-April till the first of June, with a smaller run in August some years. The number of shedders, where crabs are brought to be watched over until they shed their outer skin, have decreased these last few years. Check out the working shedding tanks that extend over the sound behind Basnight's Lone Cedar. Colington Island, on the soundside of Kill Devil Hills, has been called the "capital of soft-shells," and Endurance Seafood there still ships them by the thousands to markets up north.

How crabs shed, and mate, is a fascinating story, with jimmies and the females—sallies, sooks, or chandler's wives—playing rather randy roles. Get an old-timer to tell you.

Seafood Market Buying Tips

Clams

- Fresh clams can be stored for several days by placing them immediately on ice or in the fridge.
- Do *not* rinse, store, or transport clams in *fresh water*. Rinse them with tap water only when you're ready to cook.
- Shells should stay tightly closed or close up when tapped. Discard those that don't and any with broken shells.
- You may freeze clams in their shells, in resealable plastic bags, for up to 6 months. Shucked clams can be frozen in their own juice for up to 6 months.
- To make it easier to open uncooked clamshells, place them in the freezer for about 2 hours.
- Some Outer Bankers use this method for dealing with "gritty" clams: If you have dug them yourself (watch for official signs that the water is too polluted and shellfish harvests are not allowed), brush off sand and debris and then soak them in a large amount of seawater (i.e., water from the ocean or sound) with about one cup of added

cornmeal. This will help the clams purge themselves of sand. Then refrigerate or freeze if not using immediately.

Fresh Fish

- Always keep fish on ice, even in your refrigerator.
- Always rinse before cooking.
- Feel the flesh with your fingers to detect hidden bones, and use tweezers to remove them.
- The skin is usually removed on larger fillets by the market. However, you can easily remove the skin from raw fish fillets yourself. Peel the skin back slightly from one corner with a sharp knife, then, with the skin side down on the cutting board and holding onto it with one hand, insert the knife blade and pull it down pressing it between the flesh and skin.
- Remember the adage: Fish and guests begin to stink after 3 days.

Shrimp

- Two pounds of shrimp in their shells yield about 1¼ pounds when peeled.
- Allow ¾ pound headless unpeeled shrimp per person, or ⅓ to ½ pound peeled per person.
- When sold by count per pound, the smaller the size, the higher the counts. Jumbo means 8 to 10 shrimp per pound, large is 11 to 25, medium 26 to 40, and small 41 to 60.
- Most people prefer to devein shrimp, but it's really not necessary.

- When peeling shrimp before cooking, save shells in the freezer until you have enough to make a shrimp-based stock to enrich soups, chowders, or grits. Better yet, buy shrimp with heads on and use them in your stock.

Soft-Shell Crab

If you love soft-shells, eventually you'll want to cook them yourself. Don't be intimidated, because they're really quite easy to grill, especially, or simply sauté in butter.

How to Buy

- Make sure they're alive. Poke, blow across their eyes, pick them up to see if they still wiggle or spit bubbles.
- Do not store live soft-shells directly on ice. Place them on layers of newspaper or paper towels between them and the ice. Many markets will do that for you. At home, keep them in the coldest part of the refrigerator.
- If you have a long ride between the market and home, and must store them enclosed in an ice chest, it's best to have the crabs cleaned for you at the market.
- Purists will tell you to cook soft-shells within 4 hours of cleaning; others recommend storing cleaned crabs wrapped in plastic for up to 2 days.

OBX SeaSalt

Get a real taste of the beach with Outer Banks SeaSalt, hand-harvested from the Atlantic Ocean. Entrepreneur Amy Huggins Gaw, known as The Outer Banks Epicurean, calls herself an "accidental saltist." One day while searching for sea salt, it occurred to her that she lived less than a mile from the salty waters of the ocean. So she took a bucket of seawater and boiled it down, and burned the pot. After doing some research and her own experiments, she now uses a slow cooking and resting method, which allows the salt to have a larger grain or cube. Her salt is now sold in small jars and packages.

It's not the first time that salt has been made on the Outer Banks. During the Revolutionary War, pirates wreaked havoc, capturing ships full of supplies headed to Ocracoke and Roanoke Islands. Then a sloop carrying a large cargo of salt wrecked at Cape Hatteras, adding to the acute shortage of salt in the whole state. Salt was necessary to preserve meats and fish, so that affected food supplies. A plea was made to Congress in Philadelphia. "That's when Benjamin Franklin told the delegates to tell the good people of the Outer Banks to follow the instructions about the art of salt making in a pamphlet written by a colleague, Dr. William Brownrigg, and they would have all the salt they'd need. So the women here on the Outer Banks took their scouring pots to the ocean and started boiling it down to make salt," says Amy.

Outer Banks SeaSalt is made with the same heritage technique, in small batches without any anti-caking agents, colorants, or iodine. It's got a fresh, clean taste. It's also used in neti pots and for salt massages. Small jars and gift packages are available at outerbanksepicurean.com and several gift shops.

How to Clean

This is not a chore for the squeamish. Sharp kitchen shears work best.

- Grab the crab in one hand and cut about ½ inch off behind the eyes and mouth.
- Some love the yellow "mustard" part of the crab's digestive system; others don't. If you wish, gently squeeze to remove the yellowish contents at the edge of the cut.
- Lift the pointed end of the crab's outer shell, and remove the dead man, the gray-white gills or lungs, on both sides.
- Turn the crab over and cut off the triangular flap, called the apron.
- Rinse and pat dry, then immediately cook or store on ice in the refrigerator.

Special Produce from Around the Outer Banks

Terroir—not terror, as in pirates swarming the waterfront—is a French term that essentially means growing conditions, namely the "where," the type of soil, the amount of moisture perhaps from being close to the sea, breezes, and the amount of sunlight. North Carolina's coastal plain, particularly those counties that abut the sounds created by the barrier islands of the Outer Banks, has a *terroir* that's particularly good for melons, onions, potatoes, and peaches. Keep an eye out for these special goodies at the produce stands you'll find in several villages in the Outer Banks.

Rocky Hock melons are known among Outer Bankers to be among the sweetest in the world. These cantaloupes and watermelons are grown on the banks of Rocky Hock Creek on the mainland, near the Chowan River right before it becomes the Albemarle Sound. The "magic melon dirt," as one farmer describes it, is sandy soil that doesn't hold water, but allows the melons' roots to grow way down. With an intense sun, that's a perfect growing condition for melons. Rocky Hock cantaloupes are sweeter, like the *charentais* or *cavaillon* melons of France. Their flesh is firm and crisp, as is the watermelon, and their perfume can overtake a room.

"Mattamuskeet Sweets" is a brand much like Vidalia onions, named for the region in which they are grown. These sweet Spanish-style onions are produced from black, fertile soil near Lake Mattamuskeet where migrating tundra swans and Canadian geese congregate during the winter. They are so sweet you could eat them like an apple. If you can't make it to an Outer Banks market, go online to order at alligatorrivergrowers.com.

The creamiest creamers and white potatoes grow in Camden County, a skinny sliver of land that juts down from Virginia, bordered by the Pasquotank River that also flows into the Albemarle Sound. This northeastern corner of North Carolina is potato country, with over 5,000 acres devoted to growing the tubers. The *terroir* is similar to that in Rocky Hock, with sea breezes and sandy soil.

Currituck County is tucked between Camden County and the Albemarle Sound, and faces the beaches up past the last real road in Corolla. Take a ferry over to Knotts Island, and you can find groves of "peaches at the beaches." The third weekend in June is when the annual Peach Festival is held. Make sure you get your share of these special Knotts Island peaches, so sweet and juicy.

And North Carolina is the leading producer of the sweet potato, grown mostly in the sandy, loamy soil of the coastal plain. So you'll find variations of this favorite tuber at the Outer Banks in the form of fries, baked, or "candied" with brown sugar and perhaps topped with toasted marshmallows. Kelly's in Nags Head serves a basket of mouthwatering sweet potato biscuits with each order.

Corolla

You can drive to the end of the road, literally, in Corolla. Roll over the noisy cattle grid where the beach meets the highway, and from there north, you can only drive on the beach up to the Virginia line, past the collection of huge cottages in Carova.

"Land of the wild goose," or Currituck, was the name this section of the northern Outer Banks was given by the Native Americans. The area's first seasonal tourists, they paddled over from the mainland to hunt the millions of duck and geese that passed through on their way south each fall. Later, other hunters, mostly wealthy men from the industrialized North, came to hunt each year at hunting camps and lodges run by local guides and cooks.

The old Corolla village existed mainly to support the US Life-Saving Station and the Currituck Beach Lighthouse, both established in the late 1800s. During World War II, the Whalehead Club, which by that time was no longer a personal residence but a hunting lodge, was leased by the US Coast Guard to serve as a training base. The population of Corolla exploded from 200 to over 1,000, bringing relative prosperity to villagers as they provided for the

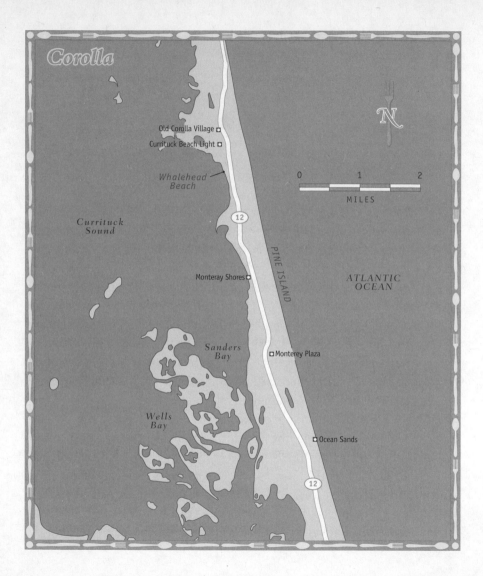

Corolla

Old Corolla Village

Currituck Beach Light

Whalehead
Beach

Currituck
Sound

N

0   1   2
MILES

12

PINE ISLAND

Monteray Shores

ATLANTIC
OCEAN

Sanders
Bay

Monterey Plaza

Wells
Bay

Ocean Sands

12

trainees. After the war ended, however, the Coasties left and so did most of the locals, to find a better life on the mainland.

By the 1970s, only 15 people were left. A few hardy tourists were adventurous enough to make the trek down from Virginia via the beach, or venture up a dirt path from Duck. But after the first paved road was built in 1975, development started.

If you build it, they will come, and tourists did. Corolla (pronounced cah-RAWL-ah) is the closest, as the crow flies, to Washington, DC and other points north, where many fans of the northern Outer Banks are from. Year-round residents still only total about 200. As a result, many of the food establishments are geared to meet the needs of a more discerning tourist and/or foodie. Now there's a major grocery store, and a bevy of restaurants, bars, and markets to choose from, but not much in the way of chain restaurants or fast food, which is a good thing. There's even nightlife, should you choose to leave your humongous "cottage." Traffic can get crazy on summer days, and you must expect some waits to eat out if you do not have a reservation.

Local soft-shells or blue crab in season, along with shrimp brought in from the sounds, are local highlights. Most places also truck in lobster and crab legs, treats that those from northern climes expect. Don't feel like waiting in line or cooking for your crowd? Corolla has several places to order good takeout, like a bucket of freshly steamed seafood.

Don't Miss

Sweet potato sticky buns at Lovie's Kitchen Table
Great coffee at Outer Banks Coffee Company

Fish tacos from Bad Bean

Fresh fish, crab balls (known as "grenades") at North Banks

To-go dishes, wines, and desserts from Bacchus

A martini from Metropolis

Foodie Faves

Agave Roja, 807B Ocean Trail, Monterey Plaza, Corolla, NC 27927; (252) 453-0446; agaveroja.com; Mexican; $$–$$$. Agave Roja offers a contemporary take on traditional Mexican fare with house-made guacamole, chicken tortilla soup, and the usual burritos, tostadas, and taquitos. Tacos are filled with mahimahi or shrimp, while the ceviche is made with fresh snapper and shrimp. A freshly made margarita, mojito, or sangria goes great with the menu. If you're feeling spirited, choose from a variety of tequilas. Enjoy the boldly colored interior and artwork, which gives the place a lively vibe.

Bad Bean Taqueria, 785 Sunset Blvd., TimBuck II, Corolla, NC 27927; (252) 453-4380; badbeanobx.com; Cal-Mex; $$. This is one of the original places on the Outer Banks that started making authentic California-Mexican food, and in the popular TimBuck II shopping complex, it has quite the following. Chef-Owner Rob Robinson worked in fancy kitchens on the California coast while soaking up the foods in local taquerias during his time off. He then returned to the Outer Banks and eventually opened this version of a taqueria.

The signature fish tacos are made with local mahimahi or shrimp and are absolutely delicious, with jicama slaw a perfect foil to the heat of the salsa, along with the just-right house-made guacamole. The slow-cooked ancho-braised pork *barbacoa* is particularly good. Quesadillas, tostadas, and hand-cut and fried tortilla chips are also terrific. Margaritas are hand shaken, on the rocks, and just perfect; there's also a large selection of Mexican bottle and draft beer. It's family-friendly, with a kids' menu. Options also include vegetarian and gluten-free.

Big Bucks, 794 Sunset Blvd., TimBuck II, Corolla, NC 27927; (252) 453-3188; bigbucksicecream.com; Ice Cream; $. I've seen kids of all ages leaving this store with big, huge ice cream cones, as large as the grins on their faces. Since 1994, they've been making ice cream, sorbets, and sherbets daily with fresh ingredients, which are then pasteurized. You can also get fresh smoothies that look really yummy. There's an espresso bar for hot or iced mochas. And order an ice cream cake for those special occasions here. Half of the store is devoted to candy and chocolates, handmade here in the Outer Banks.

Corolla Village Barbecue, 1129 Corolla Village Rd., Corolla, NC 27927; (252) 457-0076; Barbecue; $–$$. Walking around the Corolla lighthouse and the old village, you may be lured by the smell of wood smoke to Corolla Village Barbecue, located in an old building with a screened door that leads to the take-out counter. Pork is

roasted and smoked with real hickory wood, then doused with eastern NC–style, tangy, vinegar-based barbecue sauce. Get a large pulled-pork sandwich smothered with cole-slaw, or ribs, or a chicken breast doused in a sweet tomato barbecue sauce. Be sure to order some delicious corn bread and baked beans. There's limited outdoor seating, but it's best to take and go as the flies and heat can be a problem.

The Fin & Claw Sea Grill, TimBuck II, Corolla, NC 27927; (252) 453-4077; thefinandclaw.com; Seafood/American; $$$. Fin & Claw features some interesting starters, including a local crab dip and NC pulled-pork spring rolls. Look to the chalkboard for the fresh, local fish entree of the day and its creative preparation. You'll also find wild local shrimp, grilled and served over wilted greens and grits, or a scallop skillet with a bacon potato pancake, or crispy crab cakes. All natural baby back ribs and chicken breasts are grilled, along with a huge New York strip steak. The chef grows much of their produce, so expect seasonal offerings. There's a full bar and wine list.

First Light Breakfast & Burgers, 790 Ocean Trail, TimBuck II, Corolla, NC 27927; (252) 453-4664; firstlightcorolla.com; Breakfast/Burgers; $$. Start your day here with a Bloody Mary, and perhaps one of the best breakfasts in Corolla, which is served until 3 p.m.—all great for those who partied hearty the night before. The Crab Benny, with two crab cakes topped with poached eggs, and french toast made with brioche and a homemade custard, are tasty favorites. Burgers, yes, are available at lunch.

JK's Steaks & Seafood, Monterey Plaza, next to the Food Lion, Corolla, NC 27927; (252) 453-9555; jksrestaurant.com; Steak/Seafood; $$$–$$$$. Even in a strip mall, JK's pulls off a classy steak house experience. With a wood-fired grill, the menu offers aged beef, domestic lamb, grain-fed veal, baby back ribs, and chicken. For starters, try the tobacco onions, thinly sliced and dredged in Southwestern-style seasoned flour. Crisp salads, small plates, and a fresh fish entree are also favorites. There is a small kids' menu, but this is a classy steak house with a great beer and wine selection best enjoyed with grown-up company.

Lighthouse Bagels Donuts & Deli, 807 Ocean Trail, Monterey Plaza, Corolla, NC 27927; (252) 453-9998; lighthousebagels .com; Breakfast/Deli; $. If you're looking for New York and Jersey style bagels, you'll find them here, along with muffins and scones. Doughnuts are homemade from scratch daily, so that makes it hard to eat just one. There's a good array of deli sandwiches and wraps, and there's cozy seating.

Lovie's Kitchen Table, 1130-E Corolla Village Rd., right beside The Island Bookstore, Corolla, NC 27927; (252) 453-0912; lovieskitchen table.com; Breakfast/Lunch; $–$$. Located in a historic Corolla home, right beside the bookstore, this eatery/shop is a delightful spot. Get there early enough to score a sweet potato sticky bun or other homemade pastries to demolish while you sit in the swing on the front porch. For lunch, try the tomato and mozzarella panini, with homemade basil pesto, or the locally caught tuna salad, which you can have over a salad, or as a sandwich, or to take home by the pound. They also sell good old Southern pimiento cheese, and tasty wraps that you can enjoy with a cold beer or glass of wine. You'll find quite a global mixture here, as co-owner MJ trained as a chef at the Cordon Bleu in Mexico City. Her husband, originally from Italy, imports a marvelous syrupy balsamic vinegar, used to drizzle on just about everything, including ice cream. You'll also find vintage-style aprons made in Corolla, wines, and a funky selection of kitchenware.

Metropolis Martini & Tapas, 520 Old Stoney Rd., in the Ocean Club Centre, Corolla, NC 27927; (252) 453-6167; metropolisobx.com; Tapas/Seafood; $$–$$$. One of the most chic and sophisticated settings in the Outer Banks that's designed for grown-ups who enjoy drinks with their conversations, Metropolis is a hangout for locals and visitors alike that often goes until after midnight. As the name implies, they offer a selection of about 80—yes, count them—hand-crafted martinis. For scotch drinkers, the list of 20 single malts is heaven, and there's a lovely wine list as well. The owners Mark and Matt try to use as much local seafood as possible in their tapas, or small-plates menu, so the menu does change seasonally. Look for lump crabmeat fritters with lemon aioli and pickled onions, or a shrimp scampi spring roll with grilled tomato sauce. There's usually a house *crudo* plate, with cheese and charcuterie. Heavier tapas might include scallops seared and presented on a carrot puree with bok choy, or foraged mushrooms with leeks, or quail with a house peach barbecue sauce. Note that there is no kids' menu, so find a babysitter.

Mike Dianna's Grill Room, 777 Sunset Blvd., TimBuck II, Corolla, NC 27927; (252) 453-4336; grillroomobx.com; American/ Seafood; $$$–$$$$. A mainstay in Corolla, this grill was one of the first to draw a crowd for classy food north of Duck. You can get a little bit of everything here, from some selections of local seafood to prime beef steaks and natural meats. Hand-rolled sushi is served every Friday night from 10 p.m. to 1 a.m., featuring the likes of tuna sashimi or California rolls with fresh lump crabmeat. Enjoy lunch on the deck with selections that include a variety of salads and upscale sandwiches. Dinner is a bit more serious, with appetizers including classic baked oysters Rockefeller and New Orleans–style barbecued shrimp. Filet mignon or perhaps wahoo cooked over a mesquite grill, or pan-seared yellowfin tuna, and daily pasta specials are some of the entrees. You'll find a variety of cocktails and beer, and a *Wine Spectator* Award of Excellence wine list. There's a kids' menu, too. Live music rocks the place Monday through Saturday nights, and the restaurant hosts the Mustang Music Festival, held each October, which benefits the Corolla Wild Horse Fund.

North Banks Restaurant & Raw Bar, TimBuck II, Corolla, NC 27927; (252) 453-3344; northbanks.com; Seafood/American; $$–$$$. The North Banks is one of our favorites, where locals and visitors alike hang out at the long bar to watch major games, enjoy a cold brew or cocktail, and perhaps down a few raw or steamed oysters, shrimp, or clams. Booths with stainless steel tabletops and a simple coastal decor provide a relaxing neighborhood feel, where you can (but don't really have to) get dressed up. Here, the food is straightforward and delicious. Most ingredients are homemade or hand-cut, and you can taste the difference. We keep falling head over heels for the Crab Grenades, big balls of lump crabmeat, fried and placed over Asian slaw with pickled ginger and a wasabi aioli. For lunch, grilled shrimp wraps with smoked bacon, or a gamefish taco platter with the catch of the day and the typical accoutrements are always winners. One daily taco special featured local tilefish, a firm, white fish that was encrusted with a chipotle cinnamon rub, then seared; other specials included she-crab soup, and Maine lobster and crab fritters served with a jalapeño honey sauce. Shrimp cake, NC pulled pork, and grilled andouille sausage are also on the sandwich menu. For dinner, a freshly caught flounder was one daily special, served with their tasty Asian slaw, as was pasta with shrimp and scallops in a creamy marinara sauce. Both were outstanding. Crab cakes with remoulade, fried seafood, or grilled yellowfin tuna are menu standards, and there are pork chops, baby back ribs, or filet mignon if you need to get away from seafood. And of course, there's quite a variety of beer, cocktails, and wines by the glass or bottle. See North Banks' recipe for **Shrimp Salad** on p. 202.

Route 12 Steak & Seafood, 786 Ocean Trail, TimBuck II, Corolla, NC 27927; (252) 453-4644; rt12obx.com; Steak/Seafood; $$–$$$$. You'll find a bit of everything on the menu at this family restaurant that has the look and feel of a friendly roadside diner, from fried tuna or backfin burgers along with a porcini and grilled vegetable ravioli for lunch, to seafood platters, a steamed raw bar, or filet mignon for dinner. Pork ribs, bourbon pecan chicken, and Peking duck allow a change from seafood dishes. Plus, lunch and dinner specials are available daily. Pasta, pizza, and shrimp are also on the kids' menu.

Sooey's BBQ & Rib Shack, 807 Ocean Trail, Corolla, NC 27927; (252) 453-4423; sooeysbbq.com; American/Seafood; $$–$$$. Sooey's is owned and operated by the fifth generation of an Outer Banks family, and specializes in eastern-style North Carolina barbecue, made according to an old family recipe that douses barbecued pork with a vinegar-based sauce. It's piled high on plates or sandwiches. They also specialize in slow-smoked ribs, beef brisket, pulled barbecue chicken, and also Southern fried chicken. You'll find homemade desserts, like funnel cakes, key lime pie, and banana wafer pudding. There's an extensive take-out menu, with a "bulk" menu designed for small parties of 5 to 20 people. Small folks have their own "Little Piggies" fare. Catering is available, too. Additional locations located in Duck (p. 59) and Nags Head (p. 114).

Uncle Ike's Sandbar & Grill, 1159 Austin St., Corolla Light Town Center, Corolla, NC 27927; (252) 453-2385; American/Seafood; $$. Basically a sports bar with a lineup of big-screen TVs, Uncle Ike's gets rolling early in the morning for breakfast, where you can indulge in shrimp and grits, biscuits with gravy, or pork rolls, then roll right through lunch and dinner with salads, burgers, and steaks. They're known for the blackened fish tacos, hand-battered fish-and-chips, and seafood nachos. They don't close up until late, 2 a.m., and on Thursday night, there's karaoke and some nights a DJ and dancing. Kids are welcome until 10 p.m.

Pizza & Pasta

Bambino's Little Italy, 106 Corolla Light Village Shops, Corolla, NC 27927; (252) 453-4004; $$. Owned by **Cosmo's Pizza** (below), this little eatery has a very casual decor and a limited menu. You'll still find some delicious options like flatbread with goat cheese and caramelized onions, and Italian American–style pasta. There's a kids' menu and a great view of the Corolla Lighthouse.

Beach Road Pizza, 1210 Ocean Trail, Corolla, NC 27927; (252) 453-0273; beachroadpizza.com; $$. Pizzas, stromboli, and burgers, along with salads and deli sandwiches. They'll even deliver in the four-wheel-drive area north to Carova.

Corolla Pizza & Deli, 1152 Ocean Trail, Corolla, NC 27927; (252) 453-8592; corollapizza.com; $$. Fresh, hand-tossed dough for Sicilian pizza with a thick crust. Philly steak and cheese subs are a favorite.

Cosmo's Pizza, 110-C Corolla Light Town Center, Corolla, NC 27927; (252) 453-4666; cosmospizzeria.com; $$. Pizza dough and sauce made from scratch, with meatball subs, hoagies, salads, and a nice selection of beer. Cute interior with large-screen TVs.

Giant Slice Pizza, 785 Sunset Blvd., TimBuck II, Corolla, NC 27927; (252) 453-3199; giantslicepizza.com; $–$$. New York–style pizzas and specialty pies, along with hot wings. Indoor seating and some beer available.

La Dolce Vita, 798-C Sunset Blvd., TimBuck II, Corolla, NC 27927; (252) 453-0069; $$–$$$. A cute, small Italian eatery with hand-tossed gourmet pizzas, gnocchi, lasagna, and other lovely pastas, and a variety of appetizers and salads. There's a nice wine list, too.

Pasquale's Pizza & Pub, 817 Ocean Trail, Monterey Plaza, Corolla, NC 27927; (252) 453-6111; pasqualespizzaandpub.com;

$$. The owner migrated from Naples, Italy, and has been making Sicilian-style pizzas since. Microbrews also available. Families and large groups welcome.

Pizzazz Pizza, 603 Currituck Clubhouse Dr., Corolla, NC 27927; (252) 453-8858; pizzazzpizza.net; $$. Founded several decades ago in Duck, this location was added, along with Nags Head and Kitty Hawk. Call (252) 261-1111 for delivery from all four locations or order online.

Tomato Patch Pizzeria, 803 Albacore St., Monterey Shores Plaza, Corolla, NC 27927; (252) 453-4500; obxpizza.com; $$. Twenty-year-old, family-run place with Greek-style pizza, hot oven subs, calzones, pasta, salads, and seafood. On Tuesday night, kids get to make their own pizza.

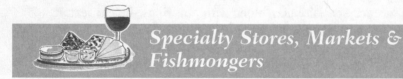

Specialty Stores, Markets & Fishmongers

Bacchus Wine & Cheese, 891 Albacore St., Monterey Plaza, around the corner from Food Lion, Corolla, NC 27927; (252) 453-4333; bacchuswineandcheese.com. A great place to provision your cottage, Bacchus offers a variety of gourmet food. There are over 750 wines from all over the world in a nice price range, with knowledgeable staff to help you choose. Every afternoon there's a wine tasting and once a week an evening tasting that pairs wine with appetizers and desserts. Choose from a large selection of imported and domestic cheeses, deli meats, and cut-to-order steaks, as well as a selection of Italian pastas and sauces. From the deli, order a great sandwich, panini, or salad. Pick up a hostess gift while browsing among the kitchenwares and cookbooks, and note that gift bags and baskets can even be delivered.

Bluewater Seafood, 501 Old Stoney Rd., Corolla, NC 27927; (252) 453-9921; bluewaterseafoodmarket.com. As they claim, you'll find "fresh off the hook, local seafood," like blue crabs, shrimp, flounder, clams, or whatever fish is in season. Order shrimp, blue crabs, or lobsters steamed, or get a Seafood Bucket to Go, which has andouille sausage and shrimp, or scallops, mahimahi, shrimp and Cajun smoked sausage, or how about lobster with king crab and mussels? All buckets include red potatoes, corn on the cob, Vidalia onions, and spices, along with the requisite cocktail sauce, butter, and lemon.

Dawn's Harvest Mart, in the field just north of the Corolla Light Town Center, Corolla, NC 27927. In season, this fruit stand carries not only berries, peaches, and melons, but also local soft-shells, shrimp, and scallops. And it will be hard to resist the homemade pies and breads.

Dockside North Seafood Market, 819 Ocean Trail, Monterey Plaza, Corolla, NC 27927; (252) 453-8112; docksidenorth.com. A satellite of the market in Duck, this seafood market features fresh fish, shrimp, crabs—some of it local—as well as steamed seafood ready to go, chilled or heat 'n eat platters, or Downeast Maine–style clambakes. This is where you can find that lobster or king crab legs that are not native to the Outer Banks. You may call ahead for orders.

Seaside Farm Market, 787 Sunset Blvd., corner of Albacore Street, at TimBuck II shopping center, Corolla, NC 27927; (252) 453-828; seasidefarmobx.com. Produce grown on the western shore of the Currituck Sound, like sweet corn and vine-ripened tomatoes, take center stage at this delightful market. And you can enjoy some freshly boiled peanuts, an eastern NC tradition, along with homemade jams and salad dressings. Some local seafood is stocked, along with king crab legs, lobster, and cod, all trucked in from the Northeast. The bakery features luscious brownies, scones, muffins, cobblers, and pies, and homemade fudge made right there, along with farm-fresh eggs and local farm cheese.

Steamer's Shellfish To Go, 798-B Sunset Blvd., Corolla, NC 27927; (252) 453-3305; steamerstogo.com; $$–$$$. Their logo says, "on the beach/off the hook," but does that mean you or the fish? Make things easy on the cook, and avoid long wait lines at restaurants, by calling ahead to this business. Some local seafood, and crab legs, mussels, and other steamed items are available along with dry-rubbed baby back ribs, roasted chicken, and vegetarian lasagna, all made from scratch. Their shrimp and scallop bisque has many fans, as does the shrimp salad. Treat your group to homemade key lime pie or New York–style cheesecake.

Coffeehouses

Outer Banks Coffee Company, 807 Ocean Trail, Monterey Plaza, Corolla, NC 27927; (252) 453-0200; obxcoffee.com; Coffee; $. This is a sweet little independent coffee shop with sugary candies available for kids of all ages, and an interesting and cozy seating area with Wi-Fi. Coffee from around the world is freshly roasted, with the usual assortment of lattes and teas. Beans can be ordered online and shipped. Breakfast wraps and sandwiches are grab-and-go, and none of the muffins and pastries are made in house.

The Shack Coffee Shop & Beer Garden, 1148 Ocean Trail (NC 12), Corolla, NC 27927; (252) 597-1500; corollacoffee.com, corollabeergarden.com; Coffee/Beer; $. Located right on the bike path beside the Corolla Post Office, The Shack is a favorite hangout. Locally roasted coffee and espresso drinks—hot or iced—and smoothies, along with pastries and snacks are served up all day. Or, when "it's five o'clock somewhere," choose from among 50 bottled and draft microbrews or domestic beers. During the summer season, live music in the Beer Garden rocks the outdoor patio, a great place to sit and admire the stars.

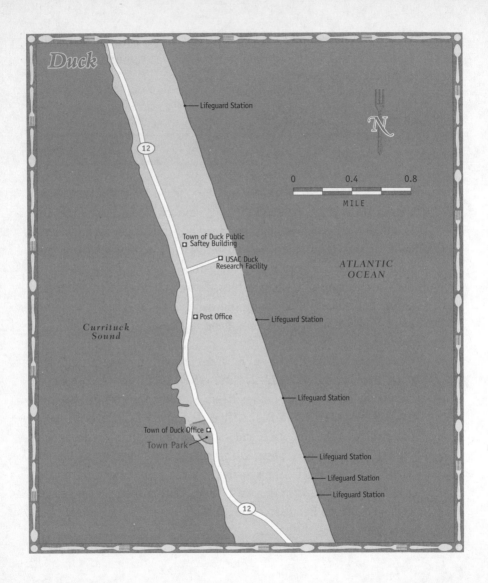

Duck

Lifeguard Station

12

N

0   0.4   0.8

MILE

Town of Duck Public
Saftey Building

USAC Duck
Research Facility

ATLANTIC
OCEAN

Post Office

Lifeguard Station

Currituck
Sound

Lifeguard Station

Town of Duck Office

Town Park

Lifeguard Station

Lifeguard Station

Lifeguard Station

12

Duck

The village of Duck requires you to slow down as you drive through, and that sets the pace of everything else in this quaint spot. The 7-mile community paved trail always has serious walkers, joggers, or bikes, and you can really shop and eat as a pedestrian among the cute shops and restaurants lining the Currituck Sound.

Duck remained a very sleepy little village on a sandy path until development started in the mid-1970s. Historically, it was a place where wealthy Northerners came to go duck hunting, especially, because of the migrating waterfowl that flocked to the shallow waters of the sound during the fall and winter.

Now vacationers flock here for the glorious stretches of beach, and for the restorative, slow spirit of the place that somehow maintains a sense of sophistication along with a laid-back attitude.

You'll find a mix of upscale restaurants along with funky places with diverse menus. There is no huge supermarket, as that request was voted down by residents, but you will find a great selection of fresh seafood and gourmet items at specialty markets.

Don't Miss

Soft-shells in season, shrimp and grits at The Blue Point
Crab cakes at Cravings
Sunset drinks and apps at Fishbone's
Coffee at Duck Cottage
Doughnuts at Duck Donuts

Foodie Faves

Aqua, 1174 Duck Rd., Duck, NC 27949; (252) 261-9700; aquaobx
.com; Seafood/American; $$$. Organic, sustainable, and natural
foods are served in this sophisticated waterfront restaurant that's
part of a day spa. The regional menu is rather limited, but you'll find
more creative dishes like line-caught fresh NC tuna, when in season,
served with butternut squash hash and wilted swiss chard and fig
balsamic compote, or roasted tilefish served with collard greens.
Braised lamb shanks have also been a cold-weather favorite. The bar
is very inviting, and since owner Lynette Sumner is certified at the
second level for the Court of Master Sommeliers, the global wine list
is quite interesting. Ask for outdoor seating, weather permitting, for
a terrific sunset view. There's a menu for "little peeps" served on a
Frisbee, although the spa-like serenity here doesn't exactly encour-
age noisy kids.

The Blue Point, Waterfront Shops, Duck, NC 27949; (252) 261-8090; thebluepoint.com; Seafood/Boat-to-Table/Southern; $$$–$$$$. The Blue Point is the premier place to catch a sunset. Located right on the boardwalk overlooking the Currituck Sound, The Blue Point, open since 1989, has a very sophisticated, sleek look that's still relaxing for lunch or dinner. Owners John Power and Sam McGann (who is also executive chef) were among the first to embrace the farm- and boat-to-table philosophy on the Outer Banks. Southern and coastal foods are presented in season, with most sourced locally. They pickle and brine, smoke and cure, and make their own sausage. Summertime, taste the marvelous shrimp and grits, done with pickled Carolina shrimp and cheddar grits topped with green tomato chowchow. Indulge in their signature she-crab soup, or a trio of Southern spreads like pimiento cheese, deviled ham, and cream cheese and pepper jelly. Late spring, catch the soft-shell crab with grits and brown butter, or pickled beets and watercress  salad with Virginia country ham and manchego cheese. Sea scallops are served with field pea "Hoppin' John," and even the mountain trout comes from a NC trout farm. Come late fall, the famed local Rose Bay oysters may float in an oyster stew. During colder months they braise short ribs or lamb shanks, and turn duck legs into confit. Pork chops, with a chipotle barbecue sauce, or beef tenderloin may be among other non-seafood entrees. Be sure to save room for dessert, for there may be warm Southern pecan pie with Kentucky bourbon ice cream, or a twist on a Southern favorite, Valrhona chocolate peanut butter tart, or a warm farm market cobbler with buttermilk ice cream. There's a sophisticated but reasonably priced wine list by the glass or bottle, and of course, there are cocktails available from the bar. During the warmer months, live music is on the deck. See Chef Sam McGann's recipe for **Herb-Onion Spoon Bread** on p. 205.

Cravings, 1209 Duck Rd., behind the Handee Hugo gas station, Duck, NC 27949; (252) 480-0032; coastalprovisionsmarket.com/ restaurants/coastal-cravings; Seafood/American; $$–$$$. Duck used to have a fast food outlet, in the form of a Burger King attached to a gas station, but when that closed, Coastal Provisions snapped up the space to offer some of the foods from their gourmet market in Southern Shores. Breakfast sandwiches are favorite starts for the day. For lunch, try the crab cake sandwich, or others made with house-roasted meats, served on their own fresh baked bread. Or the fish tacos are good. Steamed shrimp and crab are also popular menu items, and there are even lobster tails and New York strip steaks on the dinner menu. There's a good variety of beer and wine. Stick around for live music some nights.

Duck Donuts, 1190 Duck Rd., Osprey Landing Center, Duck, NC 27949; (252) 480-3304; duckdonuts.com; Breakfast/Coffee; $. With four locations in the northern Outer Banks, this business has found success with offering hot and made-to-order doughnuts as you wait. It's a great business niche that has allowed the owners, who used to be vacationers, to live in the Outer Banks. For your doughnuts, you've got coating choices, like vanilla, maple, or chocolate icing; then topping choices, like shredded coconut, sprinkles, or chopped peanuts. They offer decent coffee and espressos, muffins, and breakfast sandwiches as well.

Elizabeth's Cafe, 1177 Duck Rd., in Scarborough Faire Shopping Center, Duck, NC 27949; (252) 261-6145; elizabethsofduck.com; American/Seafood; $$$$. Elizabeth's provides lovely, romantic dining and a fantastic wine experience. Choose between a nightly prix-fixe dinner, with each of the six courses paired with a wine; or from the full menu available a la carte in the dining rooms. A small plate menu is also available at the bar and in the art gallery. There are two dinner seatings each evening, and be advised if you want to linger, choose the later one. The award-winning wine list is quite extensive, for owner Leonard Logan is a trained sommelier, and the staff is quite knowledgeable and helpful with wine pairings. Executive Chef Brad Price offers appetizers such as *foie gras* with scallops, a pecan-crusted onion torte, and the scallop and brie bisque with tart apples that keep many guests coming back. Salmon, crab, tuna, or shrimp may be some of the seafood offerings on the daily menu, along with choices of lamb, tenderloin, or duck. Chocolate *pots de crème*, smooth and light yet with intense flavor, are a favorite ending.

Fishbone's Sunset Grille & Raw Bar, 1171 Duck Rd., Duck, NC 27949; (252) 261-6991; fishbonessunsetgrille.com; Seafood/ American; $$–$$$. This is a great place to watch the sun go down over the Currituck Sound with an umbrella drink or cold beer. Don't expect sophisticated food here, as the Caribbean tiki bar atmosphere is reflected in the menu, with bacon-wrapped shrimp, or shrimp and tuna ceviche, or hot wings. Build a burger, or try a crab cake or fish sandwich. Dinner entrees include coconut shrimp, grouper cooked in a Martinique style, or tuna Oscar with crabmeat. You'll find the obligatory fried seafood, and raw or steamed oysters, clams and even snow crab and lobster. Kids have their own menu.

Kimball's Kitchen, The Sanderling Resort, 1461 Duck Rd., Duck, NC 27949; (800) 701-4111; thesanderling.com; American/Seafood; $$$$. In the fall of 2012, The Sanderling Resort closed its venerable Left Bank restaurant. After renovations and a change in concept, it's now reopened, still as a AAA Four Diamond restaurant with a new name, Kimball's Kitchen, and the same executive chef, Jeffrey Russell. What's new? A raw bar with an extensive selection of local oysters and a classic seafood tower. Menu entrees feature local, grass-fed prime steak and freshly caught, local seafood with traditional side dishes, along with artfully composed appetizers, signature dishes, and daily pasta and risotto specials. Along with a new bar menu, the wine list promises to be the most comprehensive in the Outer Banks. Live entertainment will be offered during the season on Saturday evening. Kimball's Kitchen plays homage to the superintendent of the old US Life-Saving Service. See recipe for Executive Chef Jeffrey Russell's **Sanderling Crab Cakes,** p. 193.

The Lifesaving Station, The Sanderling Resort, 1461 Duck Rd., Duck, NC 27949; (800) 701-4111, ext. 127; thesanderling.com; American/Seafood; $$$–$$$$. This restaurant at The Sanderling closed in the fall of 2012 to undergo renovations, adding an upstairs bar and lounge, No. 5, for ocean and sound viewing, and downstairs, outdoor seating. It's where most patrons staying at the resort have breakfast, lunch, or dinner, but outsiders are also welcome. Set in an actual, restored US Life-Saving Station, you'll find lots of artifacts and interesting historical photos. But the menu is contemporary and focuses on local seafood, with daily seafood specials. They're known for their delicious shrimp, crab, and corn chowder as a great starter, buttermilk fried chicken, and to finish, a marvelous white chocolate raspberry crème brûlée. There's a children's menu and also vegetarian entrees available.

The Paper Canoe, 1564 Duck Rd., Duck, NC 27949; (252) 715-2220; papercanoeobx.com; Seafood/American; $$$–$$$$. With a gorgeous view of the sunset overlooking Currituck Sound, The Paper

Canoe is a very open and sometimes noisy place that serves some local seafood with its seasonal, American menu. There are wood-fired pizzas, artisanal breads from their ovens, and a variety of seafood and pasta dishes. Most like to start with the crab and artichoke dip, and many claim the crab cakes or the scallops with succotash as favorites. Daily specials include some local fish, perhaps pan-seared with seasonal vegetables. About a dozen craft beers are featured, but the wine list is limited, and choices of wines by the glass change every week. Children are not encouraged.

Red Sky, 1197 Duck Rd., Duck, NC 27949; (252) 261-8646; red skycafe.com; American/Seafood; $$$. Tucked in a corner of a shopping cluster, Red Sky is noisy and small, and can be a busy place. I've enjoyed some lunches here, with salads and sandwiches, some featuring local seafood, like oyster po'boys. At dinner, an artichoke dip and hot bread comes complimentary to the table after your order is placed. She-crab bisque is a favorite, and seafood stew. Crab sourced from Lake Mattamuskeet across the sound is made into crab cakes, and a wood-fired mix of seafood is offered. "Ocean Impaired" is how Chef-Owner Wes Stepp lists "Duck in Duck," a slow-roasted, wood-fired duckling, and there are also ribs and steak. There's a kids' menu, but note on weekends especially, there is always a long wait with no reservations taken. **Chefs On Call,** partycateringobx .com/personal-chefs, can bring the chef and servers to your home or rental cottage to prepare a full meal (and clean up), a nice treat if you don't want to cook or go out. See p. 228.

The Roadside Bar & Grill, 1193 Duck Rd., Duck, NC 27949; (252) 261-5729; roadsideOBX.com; Seafood/American; $$–$$$. Literally right on the roadside in Duck's oldest old house, this little gem has a great list of cocktails, and artisan and seasonal beer to enjoy on the outside patio or inside at the bar. I've enjoyed some delicious sandwiches here, like the Reuben or tuna melt made with fresh tuna salad. Suppers listed are paella, pork chops, jambalaya, a vegetable napoleon, and local tuna steak with cucumber kimchee. The interior is rather crowded and small, but that can be intimate, too. There's live music some nights.

Sooey's BBQ & Rib Shack, 1177 Duck Rd., Duck, NC 27949; (252) 449-BBQ1; sooeysbbq.com; American/Seafood; $$–$$$. See listing description on p. 43.

Pizza & Pasta

Duck Pizza Company, 1171 Duck Rd., Scarborough Lane Shoppes, Duck, NC 27949; (252) 255-0099; duckpizza.com; $$. Specialty pizzas, subs, calzones, wings, and salads. Limited seating.

Pizzazz Pizza, 1187 Duck Rd., Loblolly Pines Shops, Duck, NC 27949; (252) 261-8822; pizzazzpizza.net; $$. This Duck location offers a lunch pizza buffet and outdoor seating.

The Wave Pizza Cafe, 1190 Duck Rd., Osprey Landing, Duck, NC 27949; (252) 255-0375; thewavepizza.com; $$. With a great waterfront view, this place offers beach-themed pizzas and subs, salads, along with cold beer.

Specialty Stores, Markets & Fishmongers

Coastal Provisions, 1 Ocean Blvd. (just at the turn for Southern Shores off Bypass 158), Southern Shores, NC 27949; (252) 480-0023; coastalprovisionsmarket.com; $$–$$$. Coastal Provisions is a terrific one-stop market with gourmet items, fresh local seafood and quality meats, prepared foods to go, and a wine bar and cafe. Their crab cakes are renowned, and they carry fresh oysters, wild-caught shrimp, clams, and fish, as well as mussels from Prince Edward Island. There's a nice assortment of cheeses, herbs, and spices, freshly baked bread, and fresh local produce, too. Try the chocolate pavé, a nice slab of fudgy, boozy chocolate, or other desserts. The selection of wine by the bottle is good and the price decent. At the cafe tables on the side of the market, you can indulge in a quiet meal of steamed clams or mussels, or seared scallops, or perhaps the fresh catch of the day. Or, just relax with some appetizers and a glass or bottle of wine.

Outer Banks Epicurean

Amy Huggins Gaw is the creator and energetic force of Outer Banks Epicurean, Inc., what she calls a "culinary adventure business"— like paddling kayaks around Colington Island, visiting crab shedders, and then going back to the kitchen to cook those soft-shells. She offers cooking lessons, corporate training retreats, and personal chef services, where she'll come cook in your home or rental or cater an event. She's also joined forces with Outer Banks Wedding & Etiquette Library. Reach her via her website listed below. Outer Banks Epicurean also provides precooked meals, with each dish individually packaged and refrigerated, so that you heat and eat on your own schedule. It's slow food for busy people, says Amy, who gathers her organic, locally grown ingredients from Beach Organics in Grandy, where you order and make your pickup (or there is limited delivery, too). And, she and husband John Gaw are the creators of Outer Banks SeaSalt, a marvelous white, flaky salt made by gathering buckets of water from the ocean and then working their kitchen magic. You can find that product on her website or at several of the specialty markets on the Outer Banks. See Amy's recipes for Oysters Rock-Yer-Fella (p. 195) and Sweet Potato Surprise (p. 207). (252-457-0200; outerbanksepicurean.com)

The Culinary Duck, 1177 Duck Rd. in Scarborough Faire, Duck, NC 27949; (252) 261-0455; culinaryduck.com. If you're a typical foodie, you love browsing for gourmet kitchenware and gadgets, spices, jams and jellies, and cookbooks. This delightful little shop has an interesting mix of all that, some with a coastal theme.

Dockside 'N Duck Seafood, 1216 Duck Rd. in Wee Winks Square, Duck, NC 27949; (252) 261-8687; docksideinduck.com. This family-owned market features crab cakes, she-crab soup, and NC clam chowder made in house by the crew, as well as the typical assortment of fresh seafood, most of it sourced locally. The grandmother makes the key lime pie, which is highly recommended, as well as the tomato pie, a Southern specialty. Party platters for large groups, and the precooked Down East Clambake with a combination of various seafoods, are priced per person.

Green Acre Market, right beside Dockside 'N Duck Seafood in the Wee Winks Square, Duck, NC 27949. An open-air market with seasonal, local produce.

Sweet T's, 1211 Duck Rd., Duck, NC 27949; (252) 480-2326; sweet-ts-duck.com. A cute and friendly little place for coffee or espresso drinks, perhaps with a pastry, or to browse over 200 microbrews or some interesting wines from around the world. Relax on the deck with a beer from the tap or a glass of wine, or enjoy a wine tasting one night and a tasting of brews another. Occasionally there's live music.

Tommy's Gourmet Market & Wine Emporium, 1242 Duck Rd., Duck, NC 27949; (252) 261-8990; tommysmarket.com. This foodie loves this store, in spite of the higher prices, because they source homegrown organic products and prefer buying from companies that use sustainable practices. Aged beef, and wild, local seafood are top-notch, and most of the produce is organic. Find NC specialty products, like Outer Banks SeaSalt, peanuts, sauces, jams, and edible bamboo, or in the freezer the exquisite organic ice cream made in the Outer Banks by Enlightened Palates. Shelves are stocked full of pastas, sauces, special oils and vinegars, and snacks, like salsas and homemade tortilla chips, as well as a homemade crab dip. Check out the cheeses from all over. There is a wide variety of microbrews, local and imported, as well as wines. And they have "fast food" to go. Grab a cup of coffee, a pastry, and your newspaper, or come in for a sub or sandwich. Pick up steamed shrimp, crab cakes, and side dishes for dinner, too . . . and the pie and the pound cake for dessert.

Tullio's Pastry Shop, 1187 Duck Rd., Loblolly Pines Shopping Center, Duck, NC 27949; (252) 261-7112; tulliospastry.com. Voted Best of the Beach, you can find doughnuts, bagels, fudge, and all sorts of homemade pastries behind the glass counters of this cute shop with its checkerboard floor. You can order cakes for special occasions (like being on vacation at the beach?). Enjoy an Italian ice, too. There are a few tables inside, and chairs outside under a covered walkway.

Duck Cottage, 1240 Duck Rd., Duck, NC 27949; (252) 261-5510; duckscottage.com; Coffee/Pastries; $. Yes, it's a bookstore, and an independent one, the best kind. But Duck Cottage always has a line waiting for great coffee and a variety of espresso drinks, especially during the morning. Located in an old house that was built as a gun club, you can sit on the front porch or in comfy chairs in the front room as you sip your java. Visitors return for the Coconut Crunch, served hot or on crushed ice, and the apricot walnut biscotti and other pastries. And, there is a nice selection of cookbooks!

Duck Donuts, 1190 Duck Rd., Osprey Landing Center, Duck, NC 27949; (252) 480-3304; duckdonuts.com; Breakfast/Coffee; $. See description p. 55.

Sweet T's, 1211 Duck Rd., Duck, NC 27949; (252) 480-2326; sweet-ts-duck.com; Coffee/Pastries; $. See description p. 62.

Tullio's Pastry Shop, 1187 Duck Rd., Loblolly Pines Shopping Center, Duck, NC 27949; (252) 261-7112; tulliospastry.com; Coffee/Pastries; $. See description p. 63.

Kitty Hawk &
Kill Devil Hills

Kitty Hawk and Kill Devil Hills are indistinguishable to most visitors, as they both sit "up the beach" from Nags Head, or just south of the northernmost bridge connecting this finger of the Outer Banks with the mainland. Both began as small fishing villages nestled in the hammocks on the soundside, where Native Americans set up camp while goose hunting or fishing. Later, villagers helped man and supply the federal life-saving stations, built to provide daring rescues for the unfortunates floundering in the wild ocean, known in the Outer Banks as the Graveyard of the Atlantic.

The Wright brothers lodged in Kitty Hawk while they tried to get their machine to fly a bit further south in the windy flatlands of Kill Devil Hills. During their winter trials, Orville Wright complained bitterly in letters to his sister about the lack of food available at the stores in the village of Kitty Hawk. He sounded as though he were starving.

If he came back today, Orville wouldn't know what to do with all the restaurants and food markets that are near the Wright Memorial built in his honor.

The busy five-lane road that runs from Nags Head, past Kill Devil Hills and straight up to Kitty Hawk is formally named Croatan Highway. Locals just call it "the Bypass." Commercial development is heavy along this road, with shopping centers, strip malls, and some chain restaurants. Most just use the milepost (MP) to denote their location. Jockey's Ridge, the tallest sand dune on the East Coast, sits on the soundside, as does the Wright Memorial.

Head to the ocean, and you'll find a road that runs straight along the beach, from Nags Head all the way to the north turn for the Wright Memorial Bridge. Formally named Virginia Dare Trail, locals simply call it "Beach Road," and you'll find quite a few eateries nestled among the many cottages.

Colington Road runs west along the south side of the Wright Memorial. Follow this twisty, turning road, a former cow path, to Colington Island, a sweet residential community with remnants of the fishing industry it used to support. You'll see crab pots stacked and ready, along with fishing boats tied up or "moored" on a trailer. A small sign marks Endurance Seafood, a long-standing business that still ships thousands of live soft-shells packed with eel grass up to the Fulton Fish Market in New York City. Stop at Billy's Seafood for soft-shells and other seafood to take with you, or make reservations for dinner at the sweet Colington Cafe.

During the high summer season, traffic crawls on both the Bypass and the Beach Road. Thousands of beach cottages line the

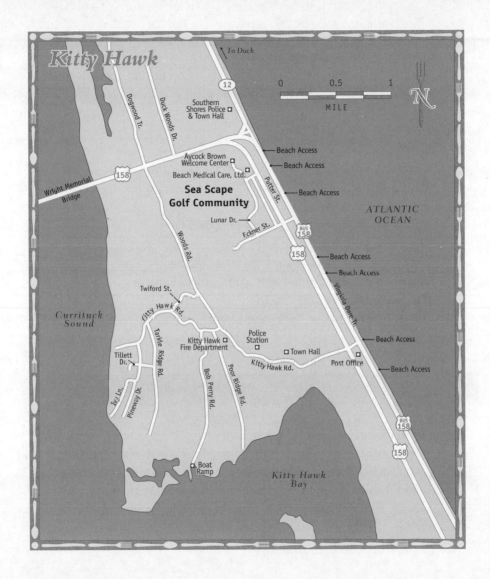

connecting streets between the sound and the ocean, most of them rented by the week. Motels serve thousands of tourists, as well. That's a lot of mouths to feed, and the reason behind the numerous eateries in Kitty Hawk and Kill Devil Hills.

Don't Miss

Zen Pops

Biscuits & Porn T-shirt with a breakfast biscuit at Citgo

Malted milk shake from Kill Devil's Frozen Custard

Any fresh fish at Kill Devil Grill

Noodle dishes up on the deck of Rundown Cafe

Fish tacos from the Food Dude

Local brew from Outer Banks Brewing Station

Country ham, sliced thin for biscuits, from Pigman's

Wine and cheese tasting at Trio

Dinner just for two at Colington Cafe or Ocean Boulevard

Foodie Faves

Art's Place, 4624 N. Virginia Dare Trail, MP 2.5, Kitty Hawk, NC 27949; (252) 261-3233; Burgers; $-$$. A great old-style burger joint, where "locals are welcomed, tourists tolerated, sometimes." Unfortunately, Art died but new owners are keeping things much the same in this tiny space. Many claim their huge burgers are the best on the beach, and their fries are hand-cut. There are also weekly

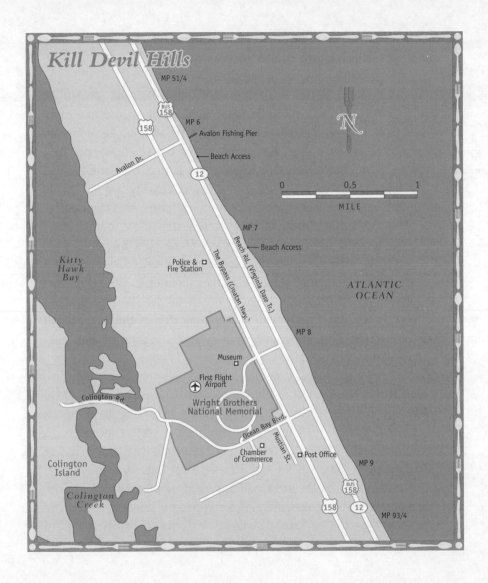

homemade meals, and standard big breakfasts. American beers are quite inexpensive here, and Hurricanes are great.

Awful Arthur's, 2106 N. Virginia Dare Trail, MP 6, Kill Devil Hills, NC 27948; (252) 441-5955; Seafood; $–$$. With a word like *awful* in the name, and all the tacky advertising you see, you kind of expect a dive. Named as one of the top-10 oyster bars by *Coastal Living* magazine, you'll find this brick-walled sports bar with big-screen TVs is actually a good family place. Known for their oysters, of course, and their oyster shooter (freshly shucked raw oyster in a shooter full of ice-cold beer, with a dash of cocktail or hot sauce), the menu also includes steamed spiced shrimp and a couple of steamed combos, crab cakes, and the usual assortment of fried seafood. Burgers and sandwiches include a soft-shell crab or the catch of the day, as well as deli meats. And, you can bet on a large selection of cold beer and a variety of cocktails.

Bad Bean Baja Grill, 3105 N. Croatan Hwy., in Seagate North, MP 5.5, Kill Devil Hills, NC 27948; (252) 261-1300; badbeanobx .com; Cal-Mex; $–$$. From Rob Robinson, the same chef-owner as the Bad Bean in Corolla, this eatery features a similar version of Southwestern, Baja cuisine using fresh, local Outer Banks seafood. Don't be put off by the strip mall or dowdy interior. Shrimp ceviche and duck confit tostones are a nice surprise for starters, or you can get the expected nachos with beans and cheese or other typical

Mexican-style appetizers. Cali burritos with slow-cooked beef brisket, or pork *barbacoa,* or marinated grilled tofu come with guacamole and a tangy jicama slaw. Tacos, quesadillas, and tostadas are of course made fresh. Bad Bean chefs make a point of using local fish, especially in the daily special; most are fillets that are grilled and served with seasonal veggies and sauce. Ribs are slow-cooked, then grilled; skirt steak is marinated with the house adobo. Not surprisingly, fresh mojitos and margaritas are among favorite tasty choices; wines and draft and craft beers are available. Save room for sopaipillas, a cloud of warm pastry dribbled with honey, or vanilla pineapple pound cake.

Barefoot Bernie's, 3730 N. Croatan Hwy., MP 4.5, Kitty Hawk, NC 27949; (252) 261-1008; barefootbernies.com; Burgers/Seafood; $–$$. Okay, yeah, with its tropical decor and music, you kinda expect Jimmy Buffet to pop out and start singing. It's kitschy, but just go with the flow and try for laid-back. As you'd also expect, you'll find cold beer and great margaritas and other umbrella drinks here, perfect for coconut shrimp, burgers, po'boys, or pizzas. One highlight is the Greek salad.

Big Bucks, 3810 N. Croatan Hwy., Buccaneer's Walk, MP 4.5, Kitty Hawk, NC 27949; (252) 715-0779; bigbucksicecream.com; Ice Cream; $. At this location, as well as the one in Corolla, there are dozens of flavors of made-from-scratch ice cream, sherbet, and sorbet. Get a big cone or have a shake, banana split, or a sundae.

There's also an espresso bar, and a huge selection of taffy, candies, and homemade chocolates.

Black Pelican, 3848 Virginia Dare Trail, MP 4, Kitty Hawk, NC 27949; (252) 261-3171; blackpelican.com; Seafood; $$. There's some rustic charm and history here, as the building, built in 1874, was used as a Life-Saving Station, and there's a nice story about a returning black pelican, hence the restaurant's name. As members of the Outer Banks Catch, they source some local seafood for their lunch and dinner menus. Pecan-crusted grouper, shrimp and grits, NC flounder, and a classic filet Oscar with crabmeat are crowd favorites. There's a limited selection of beer and wine, and a kids' menu. Save room for the Bailey's chocolate cake.

Bonnie's Bagels, 5549 N. Croatan Hwy., MP 1 (next to CVS Pharmacy), Kitty Hawk, NC 27949; (252) 255-2888; cateringobx.com; Breakfast/Lunch; $. Cinnamon rolls, french toast, and fresh New York–style bagels are made from scratch. Lunch items include Italian subs, and pulled-pork BBQ sandwiches, homemade chili, or chicken and dumplings, and tomato basil soup with grilled cheese. Catering services are also available.

The Colington Cafe, 1029 Colington Rd., Kill Devil Hills, NC 27948; (252) 480-1123; thecolingtoncafe.com; Seafood/European; $$$. Located in one of the oldest deeded homes on the Outer Banks, The Colington Cafe is nestled under the shade of huge live oak trees hundreds of years old. Dining rooms in this Victorian cottage are cozy and intimate, creating an ambience for one of the more out-standing dining experiences on the Outer Banks. Owner Carlen Pearl gathered her culinary expertise from her mother, an avid cook who grew up in the Provence region of France. Thus, the menu features local seafood prepared with a European touch and a more global style. Start with their signature she-crab bisque, or with scallops wrapped in bacon with a teriyaki ginger sauce. The fish du jour always impresses, usually presented with a delicious topping or sauce and accompanied by seasonal veggies. Beef lovers will enjoy the various seafood accompaniments, like a filet with crabmeat or fresh sea scallops. And desserts are well worth the indulgence. Many love the crème brûlée, or the coconut cream pie, served with an espresso or cappuccino. During blackberry season, Carlen picks from wild thickets on the Banks, so make sure you choose any blackberry desserts offered. There is a menu for children, but you may want to treat yourself to a babysitter when dining here.

Chilli Peppers Coastal Grill, 3001 N. Croatan Hwy., MP 5.5, Kill Devil Hills, NC 27948; (252) 441-8081; chilli-peppers.com; Seafood/Burgers; $$. At this longtime Outer Banks favorite, a steamer pot full of the fish of the day with veggies, or tacos or quesadillas with local shrimp, or shrimp and grits are great lunches you can get from their fusion-inspired menu. Local seafood is flavored with herbs from the garden. Cajun-battered shrimp and scallops, crab cakes topped with a citrus corn salsa, or half of a slow-roasted chicken are among the entrees offered for dinner. It's been voted the best place for Brunch on the Beach, and there's a tapas night during the winter months. Enjoy a game of cornhole while waiting for a table. There's live music some nights. Catering is also available. Note the owner, Jim Douglas, is responsible for developing the OBX icon and sticker.

Crabby Fries, 1006 S. Virginia Dare Trail (at the Lifesaver Shops), MP 9, Kill Devil Hills, NC 27948; (252) 441-9607; crabbyfries.com; Burgers/Seafood; $. Start your day with a breakfast biscuit or croissant, or head here for an inexpensive lunch or dinner. It's carry-out only. However, the trick is to find a spot to eat before the fried foods get cold or mushy. French fries are coated, if you wish, with a blend of spices used for crabs (thus the name). Many enjoy the Baltimore-style crab sandwich, while others like the Cuban press. Steamed hard crabs are available in season. Try the freshly squeezed lemonade and the hush puppies.

Flying Fish Cafe, 2003 S. Croatan Hwy., Kill Devil Hills, NC 27948; (252) 441-6894; flyingfishcafeobx.com; Seafood/Mediterranean; $$$. The interior of Flying Fish is a bit more sophisticated than the exterior suggests, and has a menu to match. Start off with a French martini, made with champagne, Chambord, and pineapple juice, and then move on to the scallop and shrimp chowder or maybe the tempura fried duck confit spring rolls. There's a predominantly Mediterranean style of preparing fresh, local daily catches like wahoo, pesto scallops, or jumbo fried oysters, and there's duck, steak, and more for the non-seafood lovers. An interesting wine list with some reserves is half off on Wednesday. Sweet potato cheesecake and a peanut butter "Hurricane" promise to be worth the indulgence.

Food Dudes Kitchen, 1216 S. Virginia Dare Trail (Beach Road) in Sea Shore Shops, MP 9, Kill Devil Hills, NC 27948; (252) 441-7994; Seafood/Cal-Mex; $–$$. The chef-owner of Food Dudes, Shawn Radford, is a surfer dude who has caught waves all around the Atlantic, and his menu reflects the influence of his travels. Everything is made in house, and seafood and produce are sourced locally. The cornmeal-crusted, fried mahimahi wrap with spinach, bacon, and a roasted tomato vinaigrette is divine. Also, the fish tacos are awesome. The catch of the day, like rockfish or tuna, is marinated, then grilled or fried, wrapped into a soft taco with tasty coleslaw, and served with red beans and rice. Each day, there's a fresh soup and a special on the chalkboard, like shrimp skewers over a Gouda cheese grits cake. There are some nice salads, with fish or chicken, too. Several desserts are made in house, but hope there's coconut cake. Keep in mind the dining area is small but kid-friendly (there's a Little Dudes menu), so during the evening you might have a wait. Open year-round; the Sunday brunch and Taco Thursdays are quite popular.

The Good Life Eatery, 3712 N. Croatan Hwy., MP 4.5, Kitty Hawk, NC 27949; (252) 480-2855; goodlifegourmet.com; Breakfast/Deli; $–$$. You'd better hope there's no line when you place your order here, because you'll end up staring at the display of chocolate cakes, brownies, and other tempting desserts, which can totally derail your diet. Hearty breakfasts of pancakes, crab omelets, or biscuits with good coffee are crowd pleasers; deli sandwiches and wraps are made while you wait, and on some nights, pasta specials are featured. It's a quiet place to enjoy a glass of wine or beer late in the afternoon, with one of the small plates of flatbread with various cheese or fruit toppings. Shelves are stocked with a small variety of wines, craft beers, and interesting gourmet nibbles. Note it's a serve yourself, fetch your own silverware kind of place, with lots of tables.

Goombays Grill & Raw Bar, 1608 N. Virginia Dare Trail, MP 7, Kill Devil Hills, NC 27948; (252) 441-6001; goombays.com; Seafood/Caribbean; $–$$. Kids of all ages will be entertained with the fishy decor that goes from the floor to the ceiling. The best choice here is a colorful T-shirt with their logo. Some local seafood is given a Caribbean touch, with tacos, quesadillas, burgers at lunchtime, and crab cakes, pecan-fried grouper, and other seafood on the dinner menu. Stick with the tacos and you won't be too disappointed. The bar seems to be the locals' afternoon hangout.

Henry's, 3396 N. Croatan Hwy., MP 5.5, Kill Devil Hills, NC 27948; (252) 261-2025; henrysobx.com; Seafood/Southern; $$–$$$. With a very friendly staff, Henry's is like the mom-and-pop of the Outer

Banks, proudly claiming to be down to earth, with no frills, offering "just good, simple food done Outer Banks style." So don't expect more. Although they serve fresh, local seafood, some steaks, and pasta for dinner, it's the breakfasts that are highly recommended. Here's where you can get a big meal to start your day, with country-style eggs with the usual breakfast meats, or since you are in the Outer Banks, try fish roe or fried trout instead. Eggs Benedict are served with crabmeat, and omelets come with hotcakes if you'd like. Try the Southern favorite of biscuits with sausage gravy and get a side of grits, and you'll be saying "y'all" for the rest of the day.

High Cotton Barbecue, 5230 N. Virginia Dare Trail, MP 1 (across from the Hilton), Kitty Hawk, NC 27949; (252) 255-2275; highcottonbbq.com; Barbecue; $. These local owners love to showcase local and North Carolina foods and products. Smoked for 12 hours over hickory coals, High Cotton's pork is hand chopped, then smothered with an eastern NC vinegar-based sauce. Smoked chicken is cooked whole, pulled, then sauced; beef brisket is sliced; and ribs are smoked till bone-tender. There's Brunswick stew, a traditional tomato-based stew of chicken, pork, potatoes, and vegetables. Make sure you try a slice of the chess pies, a Southern classic made in house, especially the one that's chocolate pecan. The dining room is cavernous, so it's a great place for families and large parties.

Sushi on the Outer Banks

With all the fresh fish, crabmeat, and shrimp available in the Outer Banks, you bet that you can find some outstanding sushi in a few restaurants. But remember that laid-back style? And going local? Rather than *nigiri* you might find "sushi fingers," or "seaweed" instead of nori. And instead of a California roll made with fake crabmeat, you can get a Carolina roll made with the real thing.

Here, chefs use local triggerfish, rockfish, wahoo, and grouper, all terrific in their natural state, or in ceviche, or rolled. So is the local yellowfin tuna. And although eels used to be a huge industry in the Pamlico Sound, no chef catches and smokes them anymore, so they are imported, as is the salmon.

Many of the restaurants listed below wait until after the tourist season is over before offering sushi, or only do it one night a week. The reason is because of the seasonality of the fish, and also because rolling and presenting sushi is an art and it takes a long time to prepare. I understand that each roll, even with an experienced sushi chef, takes about three minutes to make. Multiply that times a crowd and you've got a wait.

You will need to call each of these restaurants to see which night they offer sushi, as it changes each season.

Corolla:
Mike Dianna's Grill Room, 777 Sunset Blvd.; (252) 453-4336; grillroomobx.com (p. 41)

Duck:
Aqua, 1174 Duck Rd.; (252) 261-9700; aquaobx.com (p. 52)

Fishbone's Sunset Grille & Raw Bar, 1171 Duck Rd.; (252) 261-6991; fishbonessunsetgrille.com (p. 56)

Kitty Hawk:
Barefoot Bernie's, 3730 N. Croatan Hwy., MP 4.5; (252) 261-1008; barefootbernies.com (p. 71)
Sanya, 3919 N. Croatan Hwy., MP 4; (252) 261-1946; sanyaobx.com (p. 89)

Kill Devil Hills:
Outer Banks Brewing Station, 600 S. Croatan Hwy., MP 8.5; (252) 449-2739; obbrewing.com (p. 86)

Nags Head:
Taiko Japanese Restaurant, 5000 S. Croatan Hwy., MP 14; (252) 449-8895, taikosushiobx.com (p. 115)
Tortugas' Lie, 3014 S. Virginia Dare Trail, MP 11; (252) 441-7299; tortugaslie.com (p. 116)

Buxton, Hatteras Island:
Diamond Shoals Restaurant, 46843 NC 12 Hwy.; (252) 995-5521; diamondshoals.net (p. 142)

Ocracoke:
Jason's, 1110 Irvin Garrish Hwy.; (252) 928-3434; jasonsocracoke .com (p. 173)
Thai Moon, 589 Irvin Garrish Hwy.; (252) 928-5100; ocracokeisland .com/thai_moon.htm (p. 176)

JK's Steaks & Seafood, 1106 S. Croatan Hwy., Kill Devil Hills, NC 27948; (252) 491-9555; jksrestaurant.com; Steak/Seafood; $$$–$$$. Intimate and cozy, JK's is one of those classy steak houses you count on for a very special evening to celebrate that anniversary or birthday, or just the fact that you're finally on vacation and can relax. For a place at the beach, it's a welcome change from the usual seafood and seashore decor. Service is impeccable, as expected. An expansive wine list has prices ranging from moderate to special-occasion level. Aged Western beef, whether steaks or kebabs, is grilled to perfection over mesquite, and domestic lamb, veal, and duck are also choice features. Daily specials usually include a fresh catch, like tuna seared in cast iron and topped with grilled corn salsa, or tilefish broiled with local jumbo lump crabmeat and a lemon butter sauce. The French bread, by the way, is good enough to sneak home for the next day's breakfast.

John's Drive-In, 3716 N. Virginia Dare Trail (Beach Road), MP 4.5, Kitty Hawk, NC 27949; (252) 261-6227; johnsdrivein.com; Burgers/Seafood; $. This is truly an Outer Banks institution, a beach lover's favorite, and, fair warning, it looks like a dive. Set at a low spot on the Beach Road, it keeps getting damaged by storms, then rebuilt to the delight of its many fans. Fans love it because you don't have to get out of your swimsuit, as it's only takeout and a very short walk from the beach. Locals swear by their version of fish-and-chips, which is dolphin (mahimahi), battered and fried. Have it with fries or onion rings, or in a sandwich with tomato and tartar sauce. Hot dogs, burgers, and barbecue are also available. Some walk here just for the milk shakes, claiming they're the best on the island.

Jolly Roger Restaurant, 1836 N. Virginia Dare Trail, MP 6.75, Kill Devil Hills, NC 27948; (252) 441-6530; jollyrogerobx.com; Breakfast/Italian; $. What can you say about a place that has kitschy pirates all over, even waitstaff dressed as pirates? Although it might be too early in the day to hear an "Argh!," you can at least find a decent breakfast here, with huge portions, homemade toast, pancakes, omelets, and eggs Benedict with crabmeat. The dinner menu is heavily Italian, featuring local seafood. Shrimp marinara or scampi are good choices, or for landlubbers, there's prime rib. A children's menu is available for young pirates.

The Kill Devil Grill, 2008 S. Virginia Dare Trail, MP 9.75, Kill Devil Hills, NC 27948; (252) 449-8181; thekilldevilgrill.com; Seafood/American; $$–$$$. The front of this restaurant is an actual funky old dining car, listed in the National Registry for Historic Buildings. Grab a seat at one of the swivel stainless-steel stools, and enjoy a drink at the bar while waiting for a booth in the attached dining room where you can watch the busy chefs at work. The Kill Devil Grill is an all-time favorite in the Outer Banks. Chef-Owner Bill Tucker creatively presents local seafood, but without being fussy. Soft-shell crabs and shrimp are fried, crisp, and flavorful, with a house-made tartar sauce spread on the buns that makes these sandwiches truly outstanding. The crab cakes with remoulade are not

to be missed; the cheese steak egg rolls with caramelized onions are just awesome. Look at the hanging chalkboard for seasonal specials, most involving local seafood. As befitting a diner, the burgers here are big, juicy, and tasty, but you may not want to pass up the day's catch served up in a bun. The wood-roasted chicken is like the ultimate comfort food, with mashed potatoes and pan juices. And everyone raves about the key lime pie, with its buttery crumble crust and sweet yet zesty lime filling. You'll find the waitstaff here very friendly and professional. Kids are okay.

Kill Devil's Frozen Custard & Beach Fries, 1002 S. Croatan Hwy., MP 8.5, Kill Devil Hills, NC 27948; (252) 449-8181; killdevils frozencustard.com; Ice Cream; $. Local fans swear the malted milk shakes here are the best in the world. That's probably because their frozen custard is 10 percent butterfat and made with real stuff, like imported vanilla and whipped cream. Burger buns are buttered, russet potatoes are hand-cut and fried, and eastern NC, vinegar-based barbecue sauce is used on the pulled-pork sandwiches. This is "fast food" as good as it gets on the Outer Banks.

Mako Mike's, 1630 N. Croatan Hwy., MP 7, Kill Devil Hills, NC 27948; (252) 480-1919; makomikes.com; Seafood/American; $–$$. For a "fun house," entertaining atmosphere, this might be your place, especially with the kids in tow. There are sharks—mako, great whites, and not real—everywhere, and even a few small live ones in the fish tank. Count on fried seafood, some of it local, dominating the menu, but you can also get wood-oven pizzas, pasta dishes, and some meat entrees. The best to fill up on is the hush-puppy bread with onions, which is absolutely delicious when warm from the oven. Retreat to the separate bar area if you need to escape the kids waiting for their feeding frenzy.

Mama Kwan's, 1701 S. Croatan Hwy., MP 9.5, Kill Devil Hills, NC 27948; (252) 441-7889; mamakwans.com; Seafood/Asian; $$–$$$. Mama Kwan has quite a following among locals, who like to see their local seafood done with the flair that only a globally inspired tiki bar can pull off. Sure, there's a bit of Hawaiian influence, such as blackened mahimahi served with a papaya and mango salsa. But also Thai, as with the Money Bags appetizer—a wonton filled with ground ginger and shrimp, tied with a scallion. And Latino, with blackened tuna nachos and their renowned mahimahi tacos. Pan-seared sea scallops with grilled romaine hearts were superb. Burgers, grilled local tuna, and chicken are some sandwich choices on the lunch menu, along with a house-made veggie burger. And here's what gets some grass skirts going—the chocolate cake—or is it the coconut cake?

Miller's Seafood & Steak House, 1520 S. Virginia Dare Trail, MP 9.5, Kill Devil Hills, NC 27948; (252) 441-7674; millerseafood.com; American; $$–$$$. The Miller family has operated the Outer Banks Motor Lodge and fed tourists since 1978. Son Brian and his wife run

SHRIMP BURGERS

Shrimp burgers are like the Outer Banks' answer to the Lobster Rolls of Maine. They've got to be one of the best creations ever— hot fried shrimp piled high on a bun, smothered with cool and tangy coleslaw and topped with your choice of tartar or cocktail sauce. Then there's the challenge of eating it without spilling shrimp out onto the sand, boardwalk, or your just-cleaned clothes.

Check out the shrimp burgers offered at Kill Devil Grill (p. 81), or at Sam & Omie's (p. 113), or at the Sugar Shack (p. 115). Eat them right away, before they get soggy.

this Miller's eatery on Beach Road; daughter Whitney and her husband, Bryan, own **Miller's Waterfront Restaurant** (p. 109) on the sound in Nags Head. Don't miss breakfast at Miller's Seafood & Steak House. The whole family will enjoy pancakes, homemade biscuits, and sausage gravy, or perhaps a crabmeat omelet, all served until noon in this large and airy dining room. Dinner features local seafood fried or broiled, peel-your-own shrimp, and some pasta, beef, and chicken selections. Sandwiches and burgers, as well as a children's menu, are also offered in the evening. Families and large parties are welcome here.

Ocean Boulevard Bistro & Martini Bar, 4700 N. Virginia Dare Trail, MP 2.5, Kitty Hawk, NC 27949; (252) 261-2546; obbistro.com;

Seafood/American; $$$–$$$$. Don't be put off by the outward appearance of Ocean Boulevard Bistro, a former hardware store. You'll be welcomed into a rather serene and warm mix of brick walls, steel beams, and white tablecloths, with an open window into the kitchen where you can watch Chef-Owner Donny King and his crew work magic with some local seafood and other prime ingredients. The delicious rockfish swimming in a lemon butter sauce is even more delightful if you are lucky to see sport fishermen reeling in these migrating fish, one after another, off the beach just across the road. That's local and seasonal! And here, at Ocean Boulevard, you can match the different moods that summer or fall brings with both food and drink. Start your evening with a martini from their creative seasonal list. You can enjoy your drinks outside in a small, covered patio area, where live music is set up during nice weather and draws a hip, younger crowd. And the wine list is quite extensive, with some really good choices at reasonable prices. With a seasonal menu, starters can include a creamy she-crab soup that they're known for, or crispy fried oysters over greens, or a Southern favorite, panfried chicken livers with fried green tomatoes. If the tuna sashimi and poke served over shiitake wheat noodles shows up, order it. Besides daily specials, which usually include local seafood, you might find King Alaskan salmon with mussels and tapenade or perhaps a rack of lamb, pan-roasted duck breast, or braised pork shoulder. By evening's end, you, too, may lose all resolve over desserts, especially the molten chocolate cake with raspberry sauce. Be sure to make a reservation and get a babysitter.

Outer Banks Brewing Station, 600 S. Croatan Hwy., MP 8.5, Kill Devil Hills, NC 27948; obbrewing.com; American/Seafood; $–$$$. A big, spinning wind turbine along the Bypass will lead you to the Outer Banks Brewing Station, whose big claim to fame is that it's the first brewery in the whole country to be powered by wind. After a 5-year struggle over the wind turbine with the town of Kill Devil Hills, you've got to applaud them for their efforts toward renewable energy and sustainability. The idea for the brewery and "going green" started over 20 years ago, with two buddies returning from a stint in the Peace Corps in Thailand. Life eventually brought them back to the Outer Banks. In a nod to the region's history, the brewery was designed to look like an old life-saving station, with a cool bar in the shape of a life-saving boat's prow, pointed east and ready to be launched on a trail of bricks set into the floor that actually washed up on these shores years ago. The brewery is rather cavernous, yet fills up and rocks with a crowd at night, especially when there's live music. In good weather, there's a garden under the turbine out back where you can enjoy a meal or just quaff a beer alfresco. Inside, watch the brewing process through glass windows that cover one wall. A sign over the bar claims "Beer with character. Characters with beer." Among the seasonal beers available, the lemongrass beer is refreshing on a hot day, but the standard Olsch is rather decent. Try the tasting flight if you're curious about the differences in these microbrews. The food menu runs all day, and you can't go wrong with the bratwich or barbecue sandwich, both from local sources. There's the usual steamed seafood, but the crab and artichoke dip, mahimahi ceviche, and shrimp and grits are highlights. Sunday, chase away the hangover haze with their brunch, which features french toast and huevos rancheros. House-made desserts, like the carrot cake and chocolate lava cakes, are real temptations.

Pigman's Bar-B-Que, 1606 S. Croatan Hwy., MP 9.5, Kill Devil Hills, NC 27948; (252) 441-6803; pigman.com; Barbecue; $. "Barbecue" is a noun here in the South. And in eastern NC, you're talking pork that's been cooked for hours over a pit of hardwood coals, or as in the case at Pigman's, smoked with oak flavor. Pork is usually "pulled," which means it's pulled into shreds by hand, which gives it a chunkier texture, then sopped with eastern NC, vinegar-based sauce. For beef, they smoke a brisket, then chop it, then add a tomato-based sauce. An unusual offering is the yellowfin tuna, which is smoked, then flaked, with a grilling sauce and soy sauce added. Choose between combo "boats" or sandwiches, or take home containers. The country ham is sliced thinly and is perfect on biscuits. The banana pudding, a traditional Southern dessert, is scrumptious.

The Pit's Boardriders Grill, 1209 S. Croatan Hwy., Kill Devil Hills, NC 27948; (252) 480-3128; pitsurf.com; Cal-Mex; $. Probably one of the coolest places to grab some Cali-Mex food, especially

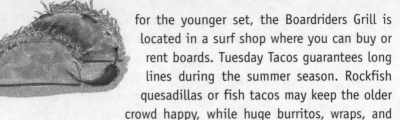

for the younger set, the Boardriders Grill is located in a surf shop where you can buy or rent boards. Tuesday Tacos guarantees long lines during the summer season. Rockfish quesadillas or fish tacos may keep the older crowd happy, while huge burritos, wraps, and pizzas will fill up heartier or younger appetites. There's cold beer, too. Upstairs are video games and pool tables, and downstairs a stage for concerts and parties makes this a popular scene at night.

Port O'Call, 504 S. Virginia Dare Trail, MP 8.5, Beach Road, Kill Devil Hills, NC 27948; (252) 441-7484; outerbankspocrestaurant .com; Seafood/American; $$–$$$. The lobby and dining rooms at Port O'Call are filled with classy Victorian antiques and stained glass, but in the Gaslight Saloon you'll find a pole for shimmying around. Although they serve some local seafood along with prime rib and steaks, Port O'Call is best known for its rocking nightlife and the live music it brings to the beach. The Caribbean tuna bites or bacon-wrapped scallops off the appetizer menu go well with a Pain Killer (a Caribbean drink). There's a long list of other specialty cocktails and wine is available by the glass or bottle.

Rundown Cafe & Tsunami Bar, 5218 N. Virginia Dare Trail, MP 1, Kitty Hawk, NC 27949; (252) 255-0026; rundowncafe.com; Seafood/Pan-American; $–$$. So what's with the name? The owners love to travel to tropical places, and in Jamaica, encountered a soup that "ran down so goooood mon." That soup became their namesake and signature dish, and consists of fish, coconut milk, tomatoes, and yams. Just recently added, the upstairs outdoor deck off the Tsunami Bar is where you want to be, gazing over the dune to watch the ocean surf or stars. The Oriental sesame noodles, a spicy mix of veggies and crushed peanuts, is excellent topped with shrimp, or the catch of the day or a soft-shell when in season. Over the last 20 years, the menu has evolved into a delightful Pacific Rim and Caribbean fusion, so you'll find fish tacos and burritos, Polynesian ginger chicken, and other spicy noodle dishes with fish or Jamaican pork. Or there's a summer bruschetta with grilled gamefish that's topped with crabmeat. If you want lighter fare, dinner salads can be topped with fish bites, coconut fried shrimp, or other choices. Brownies and ice cream, anyone? Sure!

Sanya, 3919 N. Croatan Hwy., MP 4, Kitty Hawk, NC 27949; (252) 261-1946; sanyaobx.com; Japanese/Chinese/Thai; $-$$$. Under new ownership, Sanya presents some of the best sushi on the Outer Banks. Along with hibachi grill items, the menu also offers a wide array of other Japanese, Chinese, and Thai dishes. Folks rave about their miso soup and seaweed salad; the spring rolls and sashimi have fans, too. Check out their lunch menus, especially the combos served with egg drop soup.

Stack 'Em High, 3801 N. Croatan Hwy., MP 4.5, Kitty Hawk, NC 27949; (252) 261-8221; stackemhigh.com; Breakfast; $$. The original pancake house in the Outer Banks, this cafeteria-style eatery features pancakes, of course, and also eggs, cheesy grits, omelets, wraps, and Belgian waffles that servers bring to your table. Go early to avoid a crowd. A friendly place with a loyal following, Facebook friends were asking if it had flooded during Hurricane Sandy.

Stop N Shop, 100 S. Virginia Dare Trail, Kill Devil Hills, NC 27948; (252) 441-6105; stopnshopobx.com; Deli; $. This is one of those gas stations (Exxon) where you find unexpectedly good deli sandwiches made to order behind a small, unassuming counter. There's always a line of workers during breakfast and lunch hours.

Thai Room Restaurant, 710 S. Virginia Dare Trail, Oceanside Plaza, MP 8.5, Kill Devil Hills, NC 27948; (252) 441-1180; thairoomobx.com; Thai; $–$$. The Thai Room has been an Outer Banks institution run by the same family for over 20 years. Although the decor of beads and Buddhas is a little dated, it's a favorite of locals and visitors alike who keep coming back, especially for the pad thai. Opt for the daily specials that feature the seasonal, fresh seafood, like a whole grouper fillet served with ginger vegetables or curried soft-shell crab. You can choose the degree of "hot." Exotic drinks and Thai beer are available to help cool down your mouth.

Zen Pops, 3105 N. Croatan Hwy. (Seagate North Shopping Center), MP 5.5, Kill Devil Hills, NC 27948; (252) 573-0306; pints andpop.com; Ice Cream; $. On a hot summer's day, or even in the autumn, you can bet I'll make a stop by Zen Pops. Owner and "flavor diva" Crystal Swain hand makes these all-organic, fruit-driven, Mexican-style popsicles with local fruits and herbs. Flavors change each week. *Paletas de aqua* feature seasonal fruits, like strawberry limeade or watermelon agave, and some are sugar-free, like the mango pineapple chile pop. The *paletas de crema* are vegan, made with coconut milk. Those choices always include a creamy key lime pie or chocolate coconut sea salt, made with **Outer Banks SeaSalt** (p. 29), another local product. Swain also makes Enlightened Palate, a brand of all-organic ice cream that comes in pints, also available at Tommy's Gourmet Market, Coastal Provisions, and Whole Foods markets. At the shop, you'll also find baked goodies from an Outer Banks vegan bakery, Kind Confection, like a peanut butter banana cupcake, an Elvis Week special. Hats off to Swain's efforts to keep the business as "green" as possible, like joining FatCow, a wind-powered web host, or donating cleaned, used sticks to local schools for craft projects. And, customers can place their used sticks in a bucket to "vote" for their favorite local charity; the winner gets a cash donation from Zen Pops.

Pizza & Pasta

American Pie Pizza & Homemade Ice Cream, 1600 S. Virginia Dare Trail, MP 9.5, Kill Devil Hills, NC 27948; (252) 441-3332; americanpieobx.com; $–$$. Features New York–style pizza with hand-tossed crust, with homemade stromboli, wings, and salads. Save room for their homemade ice cream.

Cafe Franco's, 1712 N. Croatan Hwy., MP 7.5, Kill Devil Hills, NC 27948; (252) 255-2232; cafefrancos.com; $$. A casual Italian restaurant with upscale pizzas, authentically made homemade soups, pastas, and antipastos, with artisan craft beers and a limited wine list. Check out their Figgy Pizza, made with dried figs and Gorgonzola cheese.

Colington Pizza, 100 Colingwood Ln., Kill Devil Hills, NC 27949; (252) 441-3339; $$. Gourmet and specialty pizzas, and a special, the Shiffletti, an Italian sandwich on a pizza. Dine in or take out and delivery available. Join them for Sunday football.

Dare Devil Pizzeria, 1112 S. Virginia Dare Trail, MP 9, Kill Devil Hills, NC 27948; (252) 441-6330; daredevilpizzeria.com; $$. Family owned and over 25 years old, this pizza place makes their dough and sauces daily. Wings, subs, good beer, and mixed drinks with big-screen TVs at the bar. Lots of seating available.

Max's Pizza Company, 3723 N. Croatan Hwy., MP 4.5, Kitty Hawk,

NC 27949; (252) 261-3113; maxspizzaobx.com; $–$$. Enjoy a personal pan pizza or the traditional larger sizes, along with calzones, fresh pressed paninis, subs, and salads. Watch surfing videos on the large screens.

Pizza Stop, 5358 N. Virginia Dare Trail, Sandy Ridge Shopping Center, Southern Shores, NC 27949; (252) 261-7867; pizzastopobx .com; $$. Serves New York–style pizzas baked in stone ovens, with hoagies, salad, and desserts. Offers gluten-free crusts. Delivers beer also.

Slice Pizzeria, 710 S. Croatan Hwy., MP 8.5, Kill Devil Hills, NC 27948; (252) 449-8888; slicepizzeriaobx.com; $–$$. Fresh New York– and Chicago-style pizzas baked in a stone oven, along with subs, calzones, and salads.

Specialty Stores, Markets & Fishmongers

Billy's Seafood, 1341 Colington Rd., Kill Devil Hills, NC 27948; (252) 441-5978. A wonderful, old-style Outer Banks seafood market, where the ladies will help you choose among the freshest, just-off-the-boat, seasonal fish fillets, shrimp with heads on or off, dry-packed scallops, pecks of oysters, and lump crabmeat. Colington Island has been called the soft-shell capital of the world, so you can bet you'll find those when in season. Hard blue crabs come by the half or full bushel. Have them steamed, with Old Bay if you prefer, and they'll even throw in some mallets to help you clean them. Call ahead and they'll also steam shrimp and oysters.

Carawan's Seafood Co., 5424 N. Croatan Hwy. (just after the split to Duck), Kitty Hawk, NC 27949; (252) 261-2120. Fresh and local, that's what you'll find at this older, expanded seafood market, like live soft-shells, blue crabs, shrimp with heads on or off, and whatever fresh catch of the day has been brought in. The price for steamed is about the same as for fresh shellfish and crabs, so I'm all for letting Carawan do the cooking and clean-up. A small selection of wine and seasonings are also stocked.

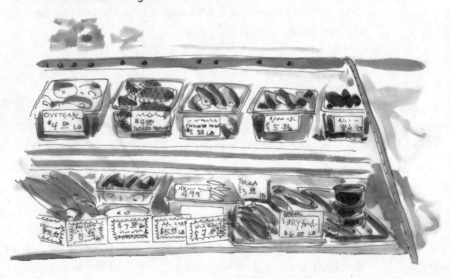

Chip's Wine & Beer, 2200 N. Croatan Hwy. (Milepost 6 Plaza), MP 6, Kill Devil Hills, NC 27948; (252) 449-8229; chipswinemarket .com. This store is like beer heaven, stocked with over 500 different bottles of beer from all over the world. And they carry over 2,000 wines, as well. Overwhelmed by all the choices? Then head to the Tasting Lounge, where they will pour you a flight of beer with a variety of cheeses, too, for a minimal price. Or, try one of the four self-serve wine stations. You'll find some cool wine stoppers, corkscrews, and other useful tools. And, they hold occasional wine classes that will help educate your palate, with tastings, of course, or you can request a private class with a group of six.

I Got Your Crabs Seafood Market & Steam Bar, 3809 N. Croatan Hwy., MP 4.5, Kitty Hawk, NC 27949; (252) 449-2483; igot yourcrabs.com; $–$$. This is blue crab headquarters. You can't beat the freshness of the crabs here, as the owner and his family do the crabbing, setting pots in the Currituck Sound. And after crabbing season is over, starting in the late fall, oysters are shucked at the bar. You can get soft-shells, crab cakes, steamed crabs, or sandwiches and plates full of crab or local fish, too. Some of the sides, such as corn or string beans, are only offered in season. Grab a canned beer or sweet tea. If you prefer, you can order crabs or oysters by the half or full bushels, live or steamed. There are a few inside tables and a long counter for eating in, but most folks take out.

La Mexicana Mini Mart, 3105 N. Croatan Hwy., MP 5.5, Kill Devil Hills, NC 27948; (252) 449-9093. Stop in for spices, dried chiles, some fresh produce, and breads you need to prepare Mexican-style foods, along with other favorite Latino snacks and cold drinks.

Seaside Gourmet To Go, 3701 N. Croatan Hwy., The Dunes Shops, MP 4.5, Kitty Hawk, NC 27949; (252) 255-5330; seaside gourmet.com; $–$$. You won't find better take-out food than this, in spite of its tiny space in a strip mall. Using local produce and seafood, they prepare entrees such as blackened black drum over a spicy vegetable risotto cake, or shrimp and crab enchiladas for you to take to the beach, or reheat at home. Vegetarians will be delighted to find many delicious options available, like artichoke- and havarti-stuffed risotto cakes, or a sweet potato and quinoa salad. The wraps are also excellent, especially with the blackened catch of the day, or with Thai shrimp or grilled veggies. Party platters, personal chef service, and wedding catering are also available.

Shrimp On The Go, 1901 S. Croatan Hwy., MP 9.5, Kill Devil Hills, NC 27948; (252) 441-0535; shrimponthego.com; $–$$. Sliders stuffed with a crab cake or shrimp salad? Voted Best of the Beach for "fast food," this former Arby's also fills sliders with tuna, Polish sausage, chicken salad, and other options. You'll also find steamed shrimp, scallops, mussels, and king or snow crab. Fried seafood is sold by the pound, and includes a few local catches. Salads, cakes, and pies will round out your meal plan. Shrimp On The Go also delivers from MP 1 in Kitty Hawk, down to Whalebone Junction, where the mileposts end.

Tarheel Too, 3105 N. Croatan Hwy. in Seagate North, Kill Devil Hills, NC 27948; (252) 441-1048. Find fresh produce, herbs, and baked goods from nearby Currituck Farms at this farm market stand.

Trio: Wine Beer Cheese, 3708 N. Croatan Hwy., MP 4.5, Kitty Hawk, NC 27949; (252) 261-0277; obxtrio.com. Trio is more than just a shop where global wines and craft beer occupy volumes of shelves, and cheeses from around the world are sweetly displayed in a cooler. You can chill out on the other side of the store in a sophisticated cafe/lounge, with perhaps a tasting plate of cheese, stuffed piquillo peppers, baked brie, or a panini, while sipping a cool brew or a glass of wine. Actually, take a tab card and a wine glass and sample from 24 self-serve wine stations, each featuring a different wine, where you choose either a taste, half-glass, or a full one. At the copper bar, there are 24 beers on tap, some of them small-batch or craft beers, or they'll fix you a tasting of three or four of your choice. Perhaps pair the dark chocolate goat cheese-cake with a dry Cabernet Sauvignon, or maybe a stout. Occasionally, there's live music.

Coffeehouses

The Front Porch Cafe, KDH MP 6, Kill Devil Hills, NC 27948; (252) 449-6616; frontporchcafeonline.com; $. A community hangout at each of three locations in the Outer Banks, The Front Porch micro-roasts green coffee imported from around the world at the Nags Head shop. Enjoy lattes, a nice selection of tea, chai, and freshly baked pastries. There's plenty of seating and a wireless bar to catch up with your online life.

Southern Bean, 3701 N. Croatan Hwy., MP 4.5, Kitty Hawk, NC 27949; (252) 261-5282; $. Locally owned, this little coffee place offers a cozy hangout for your caffeine buzz, and even a vegetarian menu for breakfast or lunch. Find delicious treats such as carrot yogurt muffins, fruit smoothies, sandwiches, and wraps, with over 30 coffees from around the world that can also be taken home.

Nags Head

Nags Head sits at the heart of the Outer Banks, and serves as the main gateway to the northern beaches as well as Hatteras Island to the south. It's home to the tallest sand dune on the East Coast, Jockey's Ridge, that folks climb to go hang gliding, kite flying, and to watch the sunset. Jennette's Pier is a fabulous new boardwalk over the sea, where fishermen spend hours casting away, couples stroll, and kids of all ages explore and learn.

And Nags Head is the old Outer Banks, where the very first cottage was built on the beach rather than on the soundside. That 1855 Outlaw Cottage is still standing, still welcoming family members to shed their shoes and their weary back-home worries, and still has holes in the floor designed to let flooding waters flow through. There are about a dozen of the original old, grayed and shuttered cottages, called the "unpainted aristocracy," that represent an era of wealthy landowners escaping summer's heat and threat of malaria by seeking solace at the sea. They brought their cooks, chickens, and cows.

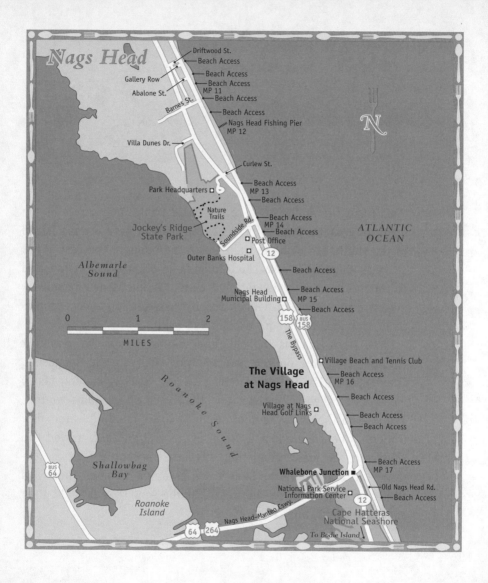

Nags Head

Driftwood St.
Beach Access
Beach Access
Gallery Row
Beach Access
MP 11
Abalone St.
Beach Access
Barnes St.
Beach Access
Nags Head Fishing Pier
MP 12
Villa Dunes Dr.
Curlew St.
Beach Access
Park Headquarters
MP 13
Beach Access
Nature
Trails
Beach Access
Jockey's Ridge
MP 14
State Park
Beach Access
Post Office
Outer Banks Hospital
12
Albemarle
Sound
Beach Access
Nags Head
Beach Access
Municipal Building
MP 15
Beach Access
158 158

The Bypass

ATLANTIC
OCEAN

N

0   1   2
MILES

Village Beach and Tennis Club
The Village
Beach Access
at Nags Head
MP 16
Beach Access
Village at Nags
Head Golf Links
Beach Access
Beach Access

Roanoke Sound

Beach Access
MP 17
64
Whalebone Junction
Shallowbag
Bay
National Park Service
Old Nags Head Rd.
Information Center
Beach Access
Roanoke
12
Island
Cape Hatteras
National Seashore
Nags Head–Manteo Cswy.
64 264
To Bodie Island

Don't worry, for you won't have to bring your own provisions to Nags Head. Today, there are plenty of great restaurants, cafes, coffeehouses, and markets to serve the thousands of tourists who find respite at this lovely stretch of beach. Good food abounds, from gracious old family standbys, to bar dives, to a growing number that promote the boat-to-table philosophy.

The chefs, restaurants, and markets that follow the mantra of using fresh, local seafood are noted in the descriptions of the restaurants listed here. With your patronage, you'll support the struggling local fishing industry, as well as find the best-tasting seafood you'll ever put in your mouth.

Here's a tip for helping you get around. The busy, four-lane highway is known to locals as "the Bypass," or "the Big Road," although the formal address used here is the Croatan Highway. Note Nags Head addresses are "South Croatan Hwy." When locals direct you to the "Beach Road," the one that runs beside the ocean, they're actually talking about Virginia Dare Trail, and again, Nags Head is in the southern section.

Don't Miss

Bloody Mary with breakfast at Sam & Omie's
Outer Banks traditional Clam Chowder at Sam & Omies, Lone Cedar, Owens', and others
Miss O's crab cakes at Owens'
Sweet potato biscuits and desserts at Kelly's
Breakfast pastries and sweets at Lachine
Fresh oysters or soft-shells or any fresh fish special at Lone Cedar

Fresh fish of the day at Blue Moon
Small plates and drinks at Brine and Bottle

Foodie Faves

Basnight's Lone Cedar Cafe, 7623 S. Virginia Dare Trail (on the causeway), Nags Head, NC 27959; (252) 441-5405; lonecedarcafe .com; Seafood/Boat-to-Table/American; $$$. When the daily specials list the name of the fisherman who caught your dinner, and the veggies and herbs come from the large organic garden growing at the entrance, you know this place embraces fresh and local. Because of that commitment, Basnight's Lone Cedar was a founding member of the Outer Banks Catch program. Order any of the daily specials, and you will be assured to have whatever was wiggling in the sound or Gulf Stream within the last day. That seasonal seafood is the primary focus of Chef Bud Gruninger, with oysters from Stumpy Point, clams from the sound right outside the window, and shrimp dragged into Wanchese. You may relish the lovely tilefish in a lemon butter sauce with shrimp and delicious wahoo with shrimp and spinach over a cheesy risotto. Chef Bud's spicy take on shrimp and grits is excellent. But there are also the usual fried seafood choices, and chicken, steak, and pasta options. Be sure to ask for a basket of corn bread, which is so yummy warm from the oven. Expect a crowd and a wait, even if you have a reservation. To keep you entertained, there's a huge wraparound porch with rockers where you can peer over the garden and watch the ospreys at their nests and the sun setting over the Roanoke Sound. The huge dining room is rather cavernous and plain, and since it accommodates large parties and children, it does get rather noisy. Grab a seat at the bar in the Osprey Lounge, where you can also eat, just to watch Ricky and Lucy, the two ospreys that return to the nest every year to raise another brood. And desserts, yes, are Southern and delicious—try the mile-high key lime pie. Sisters Caroline and Vicki Basnight have taken over this successful family business. Caroline runs the front of the house, and Vicki, who recently received her enology degree, oversees the extensive wine list that reflects her expert care in choosing those that pair well with food. Note the collection of bottles in the see-through wine "cellar." Vicki also sets and pulls her own crab pots and oversees the shedders for soft-shell crabs out back. Green-certified, they compost and recycle, use all-natural oils, and the meats are hormone- and antibiotic-free. This is one restaurant that tries to do all things right. But most importantly, they serve some of the best food you'll find at the Outer Banks. See Chef Bud Gruninger's recipe for **Pan-Seared Fresh Red Drum with Shrimp & Arugula** on p. 191.

Blue Moon Beach Grill, 4101 S. Virginia Dare Trail, Ste. 16 (in the far corner of Surfside Plaza), MP 13, Nags Head, NC 27959; (252)

261-2583; bluemoonbeachgrill.com; Seafood/American; $$–$$$. The atmosphere is casual and contemporary here and there is always a crowd for dinner. Grab a seat at the bar if you can and order the Blue Moon Margarita, a glowing blue concoction, or a brew from an interesting selection of draft beer. Chef-Owner Scott Shields and wife Melissa gained some food experience at other Outer Banks restaurants before grabbing this spot when it became vacant. I like Chef Scott's contemporary take on coastal cuisine. For a light meal, the shrimp "Not-a-Burger," mahimahi BLT, and a Caribbean pulled-pork sandwich are favorites. Fellow diners heartily recommended the creamy crab bisque with chunks of crabmeat. And be sure to try the seared scallop appetizer with sesame seaweed salad or the fried green tomato and shrimp napoleon, both awesome appetizers that you won't want to share. Crab cakes are tasty in spite of a bit too much filling, and others claim the fish-and-chips are terrific. Large, thick pork chops, served over seasonal vegetables, are deliciously tender. Non-seafood options on the menu also include a braised and stuffed portobello, a veggie pasta, and chicken or steak. Save room for a slice of key lime pie.

The Brine and Bottle, 7531 S. Virginia Dare Trail, Ste. 1D (on the causeway, in the coral-colored Caribbean Professional Center), Nags Head, NC 27959; (252) 715-1818; thebrineandbottle.com; Seafood/Farm-to-Table; $$–$$$. Just one look at the menu and you will be saying "How can I choose between so many mouthwatering dishes?" Fortunately, small plates are featured. And you can find wine by the glass or bottle to pair with each, guided in your selection by co-owner and sommelier Ashley Whitfield. Set right on the edge of the causeway overlooking the Roanoke Sound, this little contemporary bistro has quickly become a favorite among locals and tourists alike. Ashley will steer you through the list of small-production wines, or to a good selection of draft beer. She and co-owner/chef Andrew Donovan both did decade-long stints at notable New York restaurants, managing superlative wine lists and cooking at the James Beard House before returning home to their roots. This place was conceived out of their love for preserving—both the tradition of serving seasonal Outer Banks foods, as well as canning, brining, and pickling. Keep in mind that the menu changes daily. I've heard raves about the bacon jam or pimiento cheese on crackers, and the house-pulled mozzarella and preserved tomato salad. Burgers smothered in pimiento cheese, or BLTs made with the famed Benton bacon from Tennessee are favorites. The pan-seared sea scallops dishes are tops—one served with a vegetable sauté and a country ham vinaigrette and another with collard greens. Andrew's take on the iconic shrimp and grits includes cheesy grits cakes, crisply fried, then topped with tender shrimp. Desserts, such as a plum cobbler, are seasonal as well. And check out the variety of pickles and preserves for sale. And listen, folks love to peruse their collection of vinyl records while sitting at the bar, and they'll play your request. Reservations are highly recommended.

Cafe Lachine, 5000 S. Croatan Hwy. (Outer Banks Mall), MP 14, Nags Head, NC 27959; (252) 715-2550; cafelachine.com; Deli/Bakery; $. You won't be able to resist indulging in freshly made scones, fudge brownies, "Ho Ho" cakes, or the marvelous carrot cake. But that's not all that Cafe Lachine offers. Both Justin and Johanna Lachine are culinary school graduates who have had interesting careers in restaurants. Their cafe presents some terrific pastries and muffins to start your day, but it's the lunchtime menu that's most appealing. Local shrimp is crisply fried and served on a buttered bun with a spicy remoulade. Their Cuban press has repeat customers, as does the crab cake served on brioche. The Italian hoagie is a favorite, as well as the chicken salad on a croissant. Pick up box lunches or picnic baskets for two (maybe a beach picnic?), or order a side of orzo pesto or potato salad. There's a small dining area that's kid-friendly. Desserts are plentiful. Catering and custom cakes are also available.

The Dunes, 7013 S. Croatan Hwy., MP 16.5, Nags Head, NC 27959; (252) 441-1600; thedunesrestaurant.com; Breakfast/Seafood; $–$$. The Dunes has been in Nags Head for over 30 years. Renovated a couple of years ago, it's one of the places visitors head to for breakfast, especially for the inexpensive buffet that includes sweet potato biscuits, lots of fresh fruit, as well as the standard egg and breakfast meat selections. Or, you can order omelets or pancakes from the menu. Dinner is the ubiquitous fried seafood, with steaks and pasta selections too, but the fried chicken, a best seller, may be your best bet.

Fire Fly Restaurant, 2706 S. Croatan Hwy., MP 10.5, Nags Head, NC 27959; (252) 480-0047; fireflyobx.com; Southern/Seafood; $$. Deep-fried moon pie? Fried pickles? With a swamp-like decor and fireflies twinkling in mason jars on the table, you'd expect maybe gator to go with the fried green beans, collard greens, and grits also on the menu. The owners claim this is coastal Southern cuisine, and you will find some seafood on the menu. Head up to the Tree Top Bar for martinis, where there is lighter fare and tapas. There's also a kids' menu.

Fish Head Grill, 8901 S. Old Oregon Inlet Rd. (South Nags Head Pier), MP 18.5, Nags Head, NC 27959; (252) 441-5740; fishing unlimited.net; Seafood; $. You can see why this was voted the best local hangout, judging from all the folks gathered at this open-air bar and surrounding tables, based at the beachside of this old pier. It's the Outer Banks' best beach dive, with a spectacular view! Beer is inexpensive but ice cold; shrimp is steamed and a dime a shrimp; and the oyster puppies keep folks coming back for more. You can't go wrong with the fresh fish sandwich. Plus, you get to see what's being caught out at the end of the pier as the fishermen strut past. Some evenings, there's live music.

Kelly's Outer Banks Restaurant & Tavern, 2316 S. Croatan Hwy., MP 10.5, Nags Head, NC 27959; (252) 441-4116; kellys restaurant.com; Seafood/American; $$–$$$$. For almost 3 decades, Mike Kelly and his crew have presented local seafood and coastal cuisine at this Nags Head institution. Located right on the sound, the nautical decor is not too overwhelming and is rather classy. And the one food they are most known for? The sweet potato biscuits! They are delicious, warm from the oven. Before you order, note that they have won the Taste of the Beach People's Choice Award for their desserts a couple of times, so be sure to save room. Start with the clams casino, or oysters Rockefeller, or some rave about their crabmeat, artichoke, and spinach dip. There's the usual assortment of seafood available fried or broiled, or specials like broiled flounder with crabmeat or pan-seared scallops. Kelly's executive chef, John Botkin, glazes some of the Certified Angus beef steaks with a yummy bourbon molasses. And Becky Miller, the award-winning pastry chef, creates an impressive array for the dessert tray brought right to the table to tempt you with tasty delights like carrot cake and bourbon pie. The Tavern at Kelly's is also a favorite late night hangout, with live music at times, and has its own menu with lighter fare—soups, sandwiches, and small plates of seafood or steaks.

Lucky 12 Tavern, 3309 S. Virginia Dare Trail, MP 11.5, Nags Head, NC 27959; (252) 255-5825; lucky12tavern.com; Seafood/Burgers; $–$$. Lucky 12 Tavern is one of those beach dives that draws you in on promises of a cold beer, maybe striking up a conversation with another tourist or local, and a hope for a decent bite of food. With 14 large-screen TVs, it draws a crowd for NFL Sundays, especially. They have some good NC brews on tap, like Mother Earth and

Natty Greene's, as well as a long list of other beers by the pint or pitcher. Local seafood is fried, but you may also want to try the tuna bites—local yellowfin tuna rolled in Creole seasonings and then blackened—or the gooey Philly cheese steak sandwich.

Miller's Waterfront Restaurant, 6816 S. Croatan Hwy., MP 16, Nags Head, NC 27959; (252) 441-6151; millerswaterfront.com; Seafood/American; $$–$$$. A sister restaurant to the Miller's in Kill Devil Hills, this one had to be completely redone inside and out due to damage from Hurricane Irene in 2011. So there's a new outside eating area on the deck, a gazebo, and dock, perfect for listening to the outside live music some nights, and to entertain the kids while waiting. And, you can't beat the sunset view. The large and airy dining area accommodates a crowd, which means it can get quite noisy, but children are welcome and have their own menu. Miller's sources local fish, shrimp, crabmeat, and other seafood when it's available; it's your choice to have them fried, grilled, or broiled. A fish of the day gets special treatment, like red snapper with crabmeat and a diced tomato hollandaise sauce. Prime rib, steaks, and chicken are also options. The sweet hush puppies get rave reviews, as do the crab cakes with a nice red pepper remoulade. Sandwiches are available at lunch and dinner, offering a less expensive meal. There are several domestic and imported beers, some fun-looking cocktails and martinis, and a limited selection of wine.

Miss Helen's Stop Quick, 2112 Croatan Hwy., MP 9, Nags Head, NC 27959; (252) 441-6446; Deli; $. Known to locals as "Biscuits N' Porn," the small kitchen inside this Citgo gas station serves up homemade biscuits that sell out by early to mid-morning. The ladies here are also chicken experts, hand-breading fried chicken, making chicken and dumplings from scratch, and chopping up an awesome chicken salad. The banana pudding and peach cobbler are also homemade treats that will remind you of your grandmother's cooking. And what's with the name, Biscuits and Porn? This market is among the few who continue to sell porn mags, in spite of town ordinances that discourage that. You can get koozies, shot glasses, and a T-shirt that has Biscuits n' Porn emblazoned on the back.

Mulligan's, 2519 S. Virginia Dare Trail, MP 13.0, Nags Head, NC 27959; (252) 480-2000; mulligansobx.com; Seafood/Burgers; $$. Head up to the second-floor deck for a good view of the ocean and the "Unpainted Aristocracy," the historic cottages of Nags Head. Known best for their burgers, this is also a good place for breakfast. A steamed and raw bar features oysters from the Pamlico Sound, in season, or clams; other local seafood, like rockfish, are dinner features. Local produce and locally butchered meats are also featured on their menu. There's live music nightly.

Old Nags Head Cafe, 3948 S. Virginia Dare Trail, MP 13, Nags Head, NC 27959; (252) 441-1141; nagsheadcafe.com; Southern/Seafood; $$–$$$. Located in the old Harris Grocery and formerly Jockey's Rib Cafe, this small dining room is airy with a rather casual beach style, with a small bar, a few tables and booths. The menu has a contemporary and traditional Southern focus with a bit of New Orleans flavor. Try the grilled shrimp remoulade, fried pickle chips, and fried green tomatoes for starters. Low Country shrimp and grits, or a shrimp and andouille gumbo, and Southern fried chicken are popular choices, also. Portions tend to be generous. The menu also features classic burgers, fish or crab cake sandwiches, and shrimp burgers for lighter and less expensive meals. Desserts are all homemade. It's open for dinner only.

Owens' Restaurant, 7114 S. Virginia Dare Trail, MP 16.5, Nags Head, NC 27959; (252) 441-7309; owensrestaurant.com; Seafood/ American; $$$–$$$$. Celebrating their sixth decade, owned and operated all those years by the same family, Owens' offers fine dining and a chance to get out of your beach shorts and into a bit more dressy attire. That's a far cry from the hot dog stand they first started with back in 1946. The interior of Owens' is like stepping into a nautical museum, with many historical artifacts and photos, which makes it feels a bit dated. But that's not to say that the menu is stodgy. Since reservations are not taken, expect a bit of a wait. Head upstairs to the bar for a nice cocktail or cold beer. Owens' menu is focused on the contemporary coastal South, and tries to source food locally. That means a seasonal menu. You must try Miss O's crab cakes, full of jumbo lump crabmeat with very little filling, and sautéed in butter. Contemporary offerings include scallops encrusted with pecans or else marinated in Cuervo and sugar cane, or Carolina cioppino, a delicious seafood stew served over fettuccine. Or if you must, get a platter of fried seafood. There's also prime, Western aged beef, grilled to your liking. Do indulge in the tiny layer cake, a barrier island specialty of Virginia and North Carolina, that typically has anywhere from a dozen to 16 thin layers of white cake, with chocolate frosting in between each layer.

Pamlico Jack's Restaurant & Bar, 6708 S. Croatan Hwy., MP 16, Nags Head, NC 27959; (252) 441-2637; pamlicojacks.com; Seafood; $$–$$$. With a name change (from Penguin Isle) and change in concept (from more formal to casual), Pamlico Jack's provides a nice dinner experience for the family, without being too kitschy with its pirate theme. You can't beat the view here, so come in time for the sunset over Pamlico Sound. Enjoy a cold brew or cocktail on the outdoor deck in the form of a pirate ship, the Pamlico Pearl. Inside, huge, panoramic windows make you feel like you are right on the water. During high season, there's a pirate who wanders the tables and makes off with noisy children . . . or maybe just entertains them? The menu features local seafood with a bit of a Caribbean flair, with steamed raw local oysters and clams, and entrees like flounder on spinach, mahi grilled with Cuban-style black beans, or a mix of local seafood on angel hair. Ribs, chicken, and steak are available for landlubbers, or sandwiches for those seeking lighter and less expensive fare, and there's a children's menu. Wine selections are vast and have earned the *Wine Spectator* Award of Excellence, with prices ranging from reasonable to a pirate's ransom.

Pier House Restaurant, Nags Head Pier, 3335 S. Virginia Dare Trail, MP 11.5, Nags Head, NC 27959; (252) 441-4200; nagsheadpier.com; Seafood/Breakfast; $. This Nags Head institution is where you come for your Bloody Mary breakfast to "chase the hair of the dog." Breakfast includes the usual standard fare. Stick with the chowder for lunch or dinner. With a name like Pier Pressure chowder, how can you not try this? Note they will also cook your own catch for you, whether it's caught on the pier or on a boat, and they'll add sides.

Red Drum, 2412 S. Virginia Dare Trail, MP 10.5, Nags Head, NC 27959; (252) 480-1095; Seafood/Burgers; $$. Bikers and others will find a pub atmosphere and great beer for late nights with live music. A pool table and games are in the back room, and there are several large TV screens at the bar. Dips, chips, sandwiches, ribs, steaks, or fried seafood dinners are available for lunch or dinner. The fish-and-chips and seafood jambalaya seem to be crowd favorites.

Sam & Omie's, 7228 S. Virginia Dare Trail, MP 16.5, Nags Head, NC 27959; (252) 441-7366; samandomies.net; Seafood/Breakfast; $$.

One of my favorite stops while I'm in the Outer Banks, Sam & Omie's makes you feel like you're stepping back a couple of decades. Let the screen door slam behind you as you make yourself a place at the bar among the locals and fishermen from Jennette's Pier across the street. Beer is what you order here. Or if it's earlier in the day, slide into a booth and order a spicy Bloody Mary, one of the best on the beach. For breakfast, if you're lucky, native Dolly Gray Jones will be making the flat fish cakes that are an Outer Banks tradition, topped with runny fried eggs. Or there's the usual breakfast fare. Dolly's clam chowder (her mother's recipe) and soups are some of the best, and the fried shrimp burgers or fresh tuna salad sandwiches are lunchtime favorites. Fried or broiled seafood is what you'll find for dinner. And, yes, do save room for one of Dolly's pies, or plan to take one with you.

Sooey's BBQ & Rib Shack, 3919 S. Virginia Dare Trail, MP 12.5, Nags Head, NC 27959; (252) 449-4227; sooeysbbq.com; American/Seafood; $$–$$$. See listing description on p. 43.

South Beach Grille, 6806 S. Virginia Dare Trail, MP 16, Nags Head, NC 27959; (252) 449-9313; southbeachgrillemp16.com; Seafood/Burgers; $–$$. Although it looks like a hole-in-the-wall, this little place has an upstairs deck that allows great views of the sound and ocean, with a Caribbean and Asian influenced menu. Fried crab balls are tasty, as are the blackened tuna bites. Lettuce wraps are popular, and there are burgers and sandwiches. The Caribbean tuna, blackened with banana, peppers, and a pineapple rum sauce, is a favorite. Kids have their own menu for food and cocktails.

Sugar Creek, MP 16.5 Soundfront, 7340 S. Virginia Dare Trail (on the causeway), Nags Head, NC 27959; (252) 441-4963; sugarcreek seafood.com; Seafood; $$$. This scenic location used to be RV's Restaurant, and you'll find the same basic seafood menu as before. Families will enjoy the gazebo and pier for keeping all entertained. Folks like the chunks of crab in the creamy crab bisque and crab dip, and the warm corn bread. Potato skins stuffed with that crab dip, or a crab cake sandwich or burger, provide lighter fare. Entrees include broiled or fried seafood, of course, and some pasta and steaks. The **Sugar Shack,** next door in a separate building, offers sandwiches, baskets, and steamed buckets to go. In season, they fry up a great soft-shell sandwich that you will savor.

Taiko Japanese Restaurant, 5000 S. Croatan Hwy. (in the Outer Banks Mall), MP 14, Nags Head, NC 27959; (252) 449-8895; taiko sushiobx.com; Japanese/Sushi; $$. The interior of this restaurant is pretty and sleek, so unlike its mall location. Sit at the sushi bar or among the quiet tables for spider rolls, spicy tuna rolls, and other delightful hand-formed Japanese rolls. Sushi and sashimi are hand-cut in front of you, too. Or, there are so many other choices on the menu. Order soba or udon noodles or rice with various toppings, or get shrimp, chicken, and the like in teriyaki or hibachi style. Lunch specials include a bowl of miso soup, while the Power Lunch Box is served with a salad, spring roll, and seaweed salad.

Tale of the Whale, 7575 S. Virginia Dare Trail (on the causeway), MP 16.5, Nags Head, NC 27959; (252) 441-7332; taleofthewhale nagshead.com; Seafood/American; $$$. Whether you are on the deck or gazebo, or at the white-tablecloth tables inside, you'll have a nice view of the water and sunset. Start with a key lime martini or house specialty, the Flamingo Road. Or choose from a fairly decent wine list by the glass or bottle. Lighter Fare menu choices include fried, broiled, or grilled seafood, with some pasta and chicken and steak. House specialties include stuffed flounder topped with jumbo lump crabmeat, crab cakes, and shrimp and grits. Prime rib, steak, and ribs round out the menu. Both the coconut and fried shrimp come highly recommended by former diners. "Little Whalers" have their own menu.

Tortugas' Lie, 3014 S. Virginia Dare Trail, MP 11, Nags Head, NC 27959; (252) 441-7299; tortugaslie.com; Seafood/Burgers; $$. Voted the number-one seafood dive in NC by *Coastal Living* magazine, Tortugas' Lie is a great small bar with some table seating and even has a sandy volleyball court out back. It's a great place to grab a quick lunch with a cold beer. In the middle of the day, I'm afraid to try the Cayman Crippler or Shark Attack cocktails, so I play it safe with a Hefeweizen or other draft beer. One daily special I gobbled up was a huge slab of blackened tuna smeared with goat cheese, then topped with pineapple salsa. The Coco Loco chicken rolled in coconut with a tasty lime curry dipping sauce, the fish tacos, and the Swiss Jerk burger are constant favorites with repeat customers. They'll "roll you one" on Sushi Night, every Wednesday.

Specialty Stores, Markets & Fishmongers

Austin Fish Company, 3711 S. Croatan Hwy., MP 12.5, Nags Head, NC 27959; (252) 441-7412. Head just across the street from Jockey's Ridge for fresh, local seafood, like rockfish, crabmeat, clams, or shrimp in season, or find lobsters and snow crab legs, too, in this crowded, jam-packed market. Steamed seafood buckets, or just steamed shrimp or crabs, make an easy dinner to go and are worth the wait. You can also get fried baskets or sandwiches made with fresh shrimp, fish, crab cakes, or grouper fingers at lunchtime. There are a few picnic tables outside.

Cahoon's Market, 7213 S. Virginia Dare Trail (beside Jennette's Pier), MP 16.5, Nags Head, NC 27959; (252) 441-5358; cahoons cottages.com. A small grocery run by the same family for years, Cahoon's has a bit of everything. The sign out front says MEATS, TACKLE & FINE WINES. What more could you need at the beach? You'll find premade tuna and chicken salads, pimiento cheese, and a fairly decent selection of fresh produce, meats, and deli items. And yes, tackle, sunscreens, and T-shirts.

CAFE 111 PERSONAL CHEF SERVICE

When you're at the beach, the objective is to relax and chill out. And so why not hire a personal chef for an evening who will do all the shopping, prep work, come in and cook, then clean up before leaving? Sounds like heaven to me. Chef Jamie Pauls brings three to five courses you select, with appetizers and salads like mini crab cakes or caprese stacks, and entrees made from fresh seafood, like barely seared tuna, shrimp and grits, or filet mignons finished in an iron skillet. Desserts are too tempting . . . peanut butter cheesecake or blueberry pie with homemade ice cream. (252-256-2433; cafe111obx.com). See p. 227.

Crabs2Go, Wanchese; (252) 256-2922; crabs2go.com. Family owned with 20 years of experience, they fish and crab, then bring it to you. Hard blue crabs, steamed or not, along with soft-shell crabs and shrimp can be delivered free in most areas.

Nags Head Produce, 3711 S. Croatan Hwy., MP 12.5, Nags Head, NC 27959; (252) 441-9154; outerbanksproduce.com. Right beside Austin Seafood, this produce stand is all about fresh and local veggies—from asparagus to the sweetest white corn—and fruits, such as luscious strawberries from farms across Currituck Sound. You can also find lemon figs, Outer Banks Honey, or Frog Jam among the jars of homemade preserves. And, late summer, make sure you score a

Rocky Hock melon, the sweetest cantaloupes and watermelons ever, grown in sandy "magic melon dirt" in the northeastern corner of NC.

Whalebone Seafood Market, 101 E. Gray Eagle St. (near the Tanger Outlet Mall), Nags Head, NC 27959; (252) 441-8808. The Daniels family has a long history of commercial fishing on the Outer Banks. Here, you'll find fresh, just-off-the-boat tuna, cut to order, seasonal fish fillets like wahoo or tilefish, local shrimp, crabs, or oysters in season. Order shrimp or crabs steamed by the bushel in a spicy Maryland style.

Coffeehouses

The Front Porch Cafe, 2515 S. Croatan Hwy., MP 10.5, Nags Head, NC 27959; (252) 480-6616; frontporchcafeonline.com. A community hangout at each of three locations in the Outer Banks, The Front Porch micro roasts green coffee at this Nags Head location, where you can watch the process. Coffees are from around the world, but they try to source only from small, independent coffee farmers, especially those who use sustainable and organic farming practices. Roasts range from light to dark, with a variety of flavors. Enjoy lattes, a nice selection of tea, chai, and freshly baked pastries. There's plenty of seating and a wireless bar to catch up with your online life.

Morning View Coffee House, 2707 S. Croatan Hwy., MP 11, Nags Head, NC 27959; (252) 441-4474; themorningview.com. With this tagline about their coffee beans, "So fresh, you'll want to slap 'em . . . ," you expect some pretty awesome brew. And that's what you'll find in this cute, cozy coffeehouse. They use Bird-Friendly, Fair Trade certified, Rain Forest Alliance, and USDA Organic beans, a mission formed by co-owner Ashley Barnes' visits to sustainable coffee farms in Latin America. All coffees are roasted in Nags Head in small batches, from light to dark and French roasts. Blended ice drinks and smoothies are found on the chalkboard, and there are a few pastries available.

Waverider's Coffee & Deli, 6705 A S. Croatan Hwy., MP 15.5, Nags Head, NC 27959; (252) 715-1880; waveriderscoffeeanddeli .com; $. Expect great coffee and espresso drinks, as well as smoothies in this comforting spot that's a second career for Richard and Stacy Bowman, who made their vacation home permanent. Need a sandwich? They've got some great combos made with Boar's Head meats, or build your own sandwich with whole wheat or ciabatta. Then sit on the porch and watch the world drive by.

Roanoke Island— Manteo & Wanchese

No wonder the beloved, recently departed Andy Griffith chose to retire in Manteo. It's such a sweet little coastal town, worth sacrificing some time on the beach to explore. Locals, who say "Mann-e-o," can always tell a tourist because they pronounce the "t."

Walk the boardwalk that surrounds Shallowbag Bay and check out the Roanoke Marshes Lighthouse. Browse and shop in the art galleries, bookstore, and other quaint shops. At Roanoke Festival Park, see films about this 400-year-old settlement, get onboard the *Elizabeth II,* or engage in some of the supervised activities. And, you really can't visit the Outer Banks without attending at least one performance of *The Lost Colony,* the outdoor play that attempts to explain what happened centuries ago.

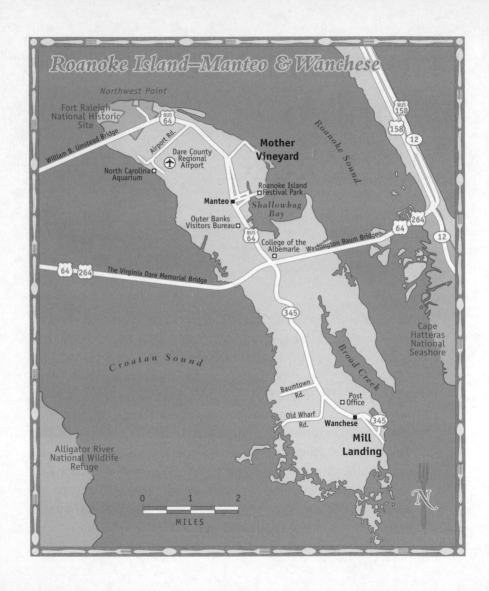

Roanoke Island—Manteo & Wanchese

Northwest Point

Fort Raleigh National Historic Site

William B. Umstead Bridge

Airport Rd.

BUS 64

Dare County Regional Airport

North Carolina Aquarium

Mother Vineyard

Roanoke Sound

BUS 158

158

12

Roanoke Island Festival Park

Manteo

Shallowbag Bay

Outer Banks Visitors Bureau

BUS 64

College of the Albemarle

Washington Baum Bridge

264

64

12

64 264 The Virginia Dare Memorial Bridge

Croatan Sound

345

Broad Creek

Cape Hatteras National Seashore

Baumtown Rd.

Post Office

Old Wharf Rd.

Wanchese

Mill Landing

345

Alligator River National Wildlife Refuge

0   1   2
MILES

N

Make sure you visit Roanoke Island Farm, north of Manteo, where costumed guides provide quite entertaining information about farm life during past centuries. The kitchen provides a look at how much trouble it was to put food on the table, and if you're lucky, you can taste some goodies cooked in the hearth.

And while you're on Roanoke Island, drive southwest to Wanchese—say "Whon-CHEESE." This is the original big fishing village on the Outer Banks, where commercial fishermen still bring in their catch. Note that the white boots that most fishermen wear are known in the Outer Banks as "Wanchese slippers." There's an industrial seafood park that continues to struggle, but you can see some huge boats being built, or see shrimp trawlers tied up to the docks, and find some great seafood for cooking or eating on the spot.

Don't Miss

Cupcakes from Carolina Cupcakery
Brew from Full Moon
Breakfast overlooking Shallowbag Bay at Poor Richard's
Sweet potato pancakes or Tiny Layer Cake at Darrell's
Fresh fish tacos from La Cabana
Best tuna salad at Annie's Great Gut Deli
Terrific soft-shell BLT at O'Neals
Outer Banks Honey, at the farmers market or some shops

Darrell's, 521 US Hwy. 64, Manteo, NC 27954; (252) 473-5366; darrellsseafood.com; Seafood/American; $$. Join the locals for a great, Southern-style breakfast here in this small, unassuming place that's been around for decades. Try the sweet potato pancakes, especially. Fried seafood dominates the lunch and dinner menus, but when in season, you can get the old, traditional boiled drum dinner, and fresh NC oysters, which have the locals standing in line. There's also pork barbecue with an eastern NC–style, vinegar-based sauce that comes from an old family recipe. Be sure to try the Tiny Layer Cake that has 16—count them—layers with chocolate frosting.

1587 Restaurant, 405 Queen Elizabeth Ave. in The Tranquil House Inn, Manteo, NC 27954; (252) 473-1587; 1587.com; Seafood/American; $$$$. You can't beat the view of the boats tied up to the Manteo waterfront and Shallowbag Bay, or the rather sophisticated, intimate atmosphere of 1587, so named for Virginia Dare's birth year. (When you visit Roanoke Island, you'll know who she is.) Start your evening with a cocktail or beer at the polished Copper Bar and peruse the interesting wine list. You'll find decent prices, until you get to the reserve wines that include some real gems. As expected at this price point, service is smooth, and the menu offers a top-notch culinary experience with seasonal and local specials. Seafood is plucked from the docks at Wanchese, the fishing village on the other end of Roanoke Island. The daily seafood special is prepared

Fish Cakes, Outer Banks Style

Don't think of fish cakes as just a way to recycle leftover cooked fish. They're a culinary treat in their own right, filled with onions, sometimes green peppers, and traditionally with cooked potatoes. The skinny cake served at Sam & Omie's (p. 113) with a couple of runny eggs over them is perfect for breakfast. And Jason's in Ocracoke (p. 173) serves a thick, juicy fish cake for sandwiches. You'll also find traditional fish cakes at Darrell's in Manteo (p. 124), Fisherman's Wharf in Wanchese (p. 125), Sonny's in Hatteras (p. 159), Basnight's Lone Cedar on the causeway (p. 102), and at the Nags Head Pier Cafe.

in a creative, yet simple manner using area produce and herbs grown on the premises. The crab cakes are often recommended by repeat diners, as is the tuna. Beef tenderloin, pork osso buco, and chicken dishes, prepared with seasonal vegetables, offer other tasty choices. Desserts, like the crème brûlée and the chocolate *pot de crème,* are marvelous treats to end a special dining experience.

Fisherman's Wharf, 4683 Mill Landing Rd. (the main road), Wanchese, NC 27981; (252) 473-6004; fishermanswharfobx.com; Seafood; $$. Eating here, in this second-floor family restaurant that peers over the harbor and sound, is like going straight to the source, for Wanchese is where the fishermen bring their catch and where chefs buy. While you wait and dine, watch the fishing boats come in and out of the channels from Roanoke Sound. The menu features that local, fresh catch just brought in, fried or broiled. Great hush puppies, warm and crispy as they should be, just may fill you up before your order arrives. Folks rave about their she-crab soup, too. Note that no alcohol is served.

Full Moon Cafe & Brewery, 208 Queen Elizabeth Ave., Manteo, NC 27954; (252) 473-6666; thefullmooncafe.com; American; $$–$$$. Sit outside when it's cool, and in the evening you just might be able to see the full moon over Shallowbag Bay. Or crowd into the cute and casual dining room and enjoy one of the Full Moon beers brewed right there. The malty Lost Colony, one of several tasty ales, hit the spot for me. Or choose from a large selection of beer from NC, elsewhere in the US, and abroad. Sandwiches, burgers, salads, and soup made daily are available for lunch. The dinner menu features local seafood, like crab cakes and shrimp and grits, or grilled steaks or duck. Quesadillas and enchiladas offer a more moderately priced but tasty alternative.

Great Gut Deli, 218 Thicket Lump Rd., Wanchese, NC 27981; (252) 473-2479; Seafood/Deli; $. This is a hidden gem of a place along the Wanchese waterfront, or specifically, the Great Gut, where the road and sound curve away from most of the development. The locals know, and that's where they head for lunch. Sandwiches include whatever's the fish of the day, plus there's homemade soup,

THE MOTHER VINEYARD

A huge, knobby set of trunks, twisted and deformed, entwine under a massive maze of trellises that support the oldest cultivated grapevine in the United States. Believed to be over 400 years old, this Mother Vineyard, as it is known, is now surrounded by quiet suburban homes on a back street of Manteo near Shallowbag Bay.

Sir Walter Raleigh's explorers reported in 1584 that Muscadine vines on Roanoke Island "covered every shrub and climbed the tops of high cedars. In all the world, a similar abundance was not to be found."

Who planted the vines that make up the Mother Vineyard an equal distance apart? The earliest settlers reported that the Croatans of the Algonquians made and enjoyed wine, and we now know they had enough agricultural knowledge to produce hybrids, use natural fertilizers, and use scaffolding to protect their other crops. Or did the Lost Colonists, using their planter's knowledge, cultivate the wild vines growing on the island?

The Mother Vineyard is a rare albino Muscadine that produces white grapes, similar to the bronze Muscadine, or Scuppernong, which thrives all over the hot, humid coastal plain of North Carolina and is used for jellies, pies, and cakes as well as wine. A few years ago, the vineyard was accidentally sprayed with an herbicide and part of it died. The whole state mourned, but with guidance from specialists, it has been nurtured back to health.

terrific tuna salad made from freshly caught and roasted tuna, and there are unexpected daily treats like the Cuban press sub or a Monte Cristo or a panini on grilled flatbread.

La Cabana, 112 Hwy. 64/264, Manteo, NC 27954; (252) 473-9364; lacabanaobx.com; Latino; $. A most pleasant surprise, this small and friendly restaurant features Latino food that's not necessarily Mexican but from all across Central America. The owners are from Belize, and delight in offering their spin on fresh local seafood, as well as specialties such as Guatemalan chicken, Salvadoran *pupusas,* or Honduran fried fish with fried green plantains. Folks rave about the salsa served with the fresh tortilla chips, and the Belize-style potato salad. Tender and delelctable, the Cuban-style stewed chicken is another crowd pleaser. More familiar Latino foods, such as tamales, chimichangas, or fajitas will also delight your taste buds.

Ortega'z Southwest Grill, 201 Sir Walter Raleigh St., Manteo, NC 27954; (252) 473-5911; ortegaz.com; Latino; $$–$$$. With its cool tile floor, Southwestern art, and colored walls, Ortega'z is a welcome diversity to the Outer Banks' culinary scene. Run by a friendly duo, a former Coast Guarder, Lisa, and her husband Marcelo, from Santiago, Chile, Ortega'z offers a delightful menu that includes local seafood and produce prepared in a Southwestern style. As expected, fajitas, tacos, ceviche, and enchiladas dominate, but there are also wraps from pulled pork or steak, or pasta, brochettes, or even seafood paella. Margaritas are house-made, and there's a decent selection of brews and wines, too. A small outdoor patio can be pleasant, minus the heat and mosquitoes.

Poor Richard's Sandwich Shop, 303 Queen Elizabeth Ave., Manteo, NC 27954; (252) 473-3333; poorrichardsmanteo.com; Deli/Burgers; $–$$. This funky little shop is the perfect place to start the day with a good breakfast. Homemade sweet potato biscuits with bacon, egg, and cheese, or any standard egg combos can be taken on the outside deck to watch the boat activity on the waterfront. There's a great selection of sandwiches and wraps made while you wait, and a few soups and salads, too. It's a small place where young and old crowd in for live music or karaoke some evenings and enjoy a few brews.

Pizza & Pasta

Island Garden Deli & Pizzeria, 512 S. US Hwy. 64, Manteo, NC 27954; (252) 473-6888; gardenpizzeria.com; $–$$. New York–style, hand-tossed pizzas, with subs made with freshly baked rolls. House-made chicken or tuna salad, paninis, burgers, and salads are also available. Eat in or out on the porch.

Carolina Cupcakery, 205 Budleigh St., Manteo, NC 27954; (252) 305-8501; carolinacupcakery.com. Walking into a storefront that has rows and rows of decorated cupcakes brings out the kid in all of us. Delightful in taste and appearance, these homemade cupcakes are made with Amish butter, local produce, or fair-trade chocolate in a seemingly endless variety of flavors. You can get gluten-free, low-carb, or vegan varieties, too. Kahlua and cream seem to be brides' favorites, while the dark chocolate infused with habañero and cinnamon spice is another. You'll fall for the chocolate coma with brownie batter and ganache. Cupcakes can be ordered ahead for birthdays, weddings, or just for fun.

Coastal Farmers Co-Op, 110 Fernando St., Manteo, NC 27954; (252) 370-6367; (on Facebook). This co-op of a dozen farmers and producers offers CSA shares, but also stocks this tiny little market with produce, eggs, honey, and some meats, grains, and gifts. Check their Facebook page for what's in stock.

Manteo Farmers Market, George Washington Creef Park, on Manteo's waterfront, Saturday only, 8 a.m. until noon. You'll find several area farmers or distributors selling local veggies and fruits, along with jams, honey, pastries, and lots of crafts under the shade of the big live oak trees. Look for Outer Banks Honey, whose bees gather nectar from the growth near sounds and backwaters, or the sweetest cantaloupes from Rocky Hock, or sweet onions from the black soil of Mattamuskeet.

O'Neals Sea Harvest Market & Cafe, 622 Harbor Rd., in the Wanchese Seafood Industrial Park; (252) 473-4535; onealsseaharvest .com; $. O'Neal's is a two-for-one hit in anyone's book. This is where fishermen and crabbers unload their catch, and you will want to stock up here on crabmeat or soft-shells in season, or shrimp, or any of the local fish. Ice is freely provided to pack coolers. Plan your stop to coincide with lunch, for they've added a terrific kitchen, where they'll fry up shrimp, fish of the day, or soft-shells, along with chicken or rib eye, for a basket or sandwich with fries or better yet, fried okra. There's seating indoors or on the porch.

Coffeehouses

The Coffeehouse on Roanoke Island, 106 Sir Walter Raleigh St., Manteo, NC 27954; (252) 475-1295; $. This is a quintessential coffeehouse, a cozy place to catch a hot or iced cup of coffee, espresso, or tea, and even smoothies. There are muffins and pastries baked in house, and some gifts. But the best part of this coffee shop is the clutch of locals who meet and greet every morning in the comfy seating inside. They'll fill you in on what's happening around town, or not, depending on your own demeanor. Or enjoy the small cafe tables overlooking the street.

The Front Porch Cafe, 300 US Hwy. 64, Manteo, NC 27954; (252) 473-3160; frontporchcafeonline.com; $. One of four coffee houses for Kill Devil Coffee Roasters, The Front Porch offers terrific freshly roasted coffees from small, sustainable coffee farmers from around the world. The dark roasts are sublime, or try one of the many espresso drinks, or enjoy some tea or hot chocolate. Muffins, bagels, and other pastries are baked on the premises. Lots of tables, a counter full of electrical outlets, and a few sofas allow many to comfortably enjoy free Wi-Fi access.

Hatteras Island

Mention Hatteras to any fisherman, and a wistful look will wash over his face, for Hatteras Island is a fishing mecca. Among the first places on the East Coast to establish a fishing charter industry, it's known as the sportfishing capital of the world. During late afternoons, you can catch the boats at the Oregon Inlet Fishing Center, or down at the docks at Hatteras Village, as they return from a day offshore. Boat hands toss their catch onto the boardwalk, and the paying fishermen gleefully pose for photos with their trophies, before the fish are gathered and wheeled to the cleaning station.

Surf fishing at the Cape, that great elbow sticking way out almost to the Gulf Stream, is also superb. On days when driving on the beach is permitted, you'll see hundreds of trucks parked with their tailgates at the ocean's edge, fishing poles standing at attention, waiting for strikes from bluefish, rockfish, drums, or other good-tasting specimens migrating by. Before fires were banned from the beach, those fishermen would grill their catch, an immediate reward for all those casts into the surf.

Drive over the Bonner Bridge, which looms over the gorgeous, ever-moving Oregon Inlet, and you'll find seemingly endless miles

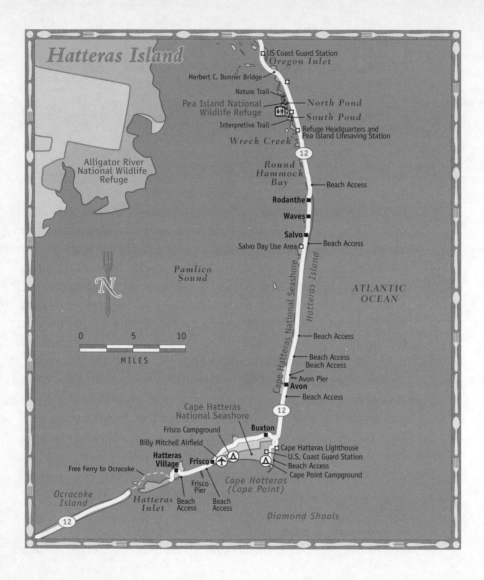

Hatteras Island

US Coast Guard Station
Oregon Inlet

Herbert C. Bonner Bridge

Nature Trail

Pea Island National
Wildlife Refuge

North Pond

South Pond

Interpretive Trail

Refuge Headquarters and
Pea Island Lifesaving Station

Wreck Creek

12

Round
Hammock
Bay

Beach Access

Rodanthe

Waves

Salvo

Salvo Day Use Area

Beach Access

Alligator River
National Wildlife
Refuge

Pamlico
Sound

Cape Hatteras National Seashore

Hatteras Island

ATLANTIC
OCEAN

N

0   5   10
MILES

Beach Access

Beach Access
Beach Access

Avon Pier

Avon

Beach Access

12

Cape Hatteras
National Seashore

Frisco Campground

Billy Mitchell Airfield

Buxton

Cape Hatteras Lighthouse

U.S. Coast Guard Station

Beach Access

Cape Point Campground

Hatteras
Village

Frisco

Free Ferry to Ocracoke

Frisco
Pier

Cape Hatteras
(Cape Point)

Ocracoke
Island

12

Hatteras
Inlet

Beach
Access

Beach
Access

Diamond Shoals

of nothing but sand and the sea until you get to the first of seven villages on Hatteras Island. About 75 percent of the island is undeveloped National Park Service property, including Pea Island National Wildlife Refuge. Hurricanes and nor'easters wreak havoc with these villages and the inlet, and particularly the NC 12 Highway, the narrow, two-lane strip of asphalt that connects the island with the rest of the world.

On those 60 long miles of windswept, white-sand beaches, sometimes there are no other souls within sight. On the other side of this narrow island, duck blinds stand out in the middle of Pamlico Sound, where hunters wait for the migrating birds during cold weather. Wind and kite surfers also flock to these shallow waters, where they whizz along the water at frightening speeds, entertaining onlookers with their acrobatics, and antagonizing those trying to harvest from the shallows, too. You'll see some clam diggers with their rakes, dragging floating baskets behind them, crabbers hauling pots and emptying them into baskets on their boats, and fishermen hauling nets from the stakes, or pound nets, left in the sound.

The waters here have provided sustenance since Native Americans, and then settlers, made their homes in high hammocks along the sound.

Historically isolated, without much fertile garden soil, Hatteras Island natives still ate well. Oysters and clams, blue crabs and soft-shells, and flounder and a whole variety of finfish came from the sounds. Hatteras-style chowder, chock-full of chopped clams, onions, and potatoes, seasoned with black pepper, was cooked in a clear broth, for no milk or cream was readily available. When huge drum fish were caught in the surf, an entire village could be fed with the boiled fish and potatoes. Stewed crabs covered with "pie bread" still grace family gatherings. Fish cakes made from leftovers, opened clams or oysters baked with breadcrumbs, and delicate crab cakes have traditionally fed many Hatteras natives.

Commercial fishermen continue to head out through the shoaling and shifting Oregon Inlet or the smaller Hatteras Inlet to net and catch wahoo, grouper, and mahimahi out in the Gulf Stream, just 40 minutes away. But they also continue to struggle financially and with the weather to bring their catch from their boats to our tables. That's why those restaurants that make the effort to source their seafood from local fishermen are noted in the Foodie Faves that follow.

While many restaurants on Hatteras Island continue to offer the traditional breaded and fried versions of seafood, you will also find a few of the restaurants listed here that present shrimp or oysters or fish with a delicious contemporary twist. And that makes for good eating, too.

For convenience, the restaurants and markets listed here have been divided into the northern villages of Rodanthe, Waves, Salvo, Avon, then Buxton and Frisco, and then Hatteras Village at the southern tip of the island.

The Northern Villages

Rodanthe is the first village you'll enter from the north, then Waves and Salvo, an area sometimes referred to by Realtors as the Tri-Village. You'll find restaurants, gas stations, and tackle shops in each. After another long stretch of nothing but beach is the village of Avon, first named by Native Americans "Kinnakeet," and where you'll find more stores and even a movie theater. Buxton has the most commercial development, and that's at the widest part of the island, at the crook of the elbow where Cape Hatteras juts out and where the famed black and white striped lighthouse towers over its new location. This is surf fishing territory. And Frisco is just below, and that's where you'll find a Native American museum and a great tackle shop.

During the last couple of years, Hurricanes Irene and Sandy washed over the highway and much flooding and damage occurred. But Hatteras residents are a hardy and optimistic bunch, and they continue to rebuild and revive their homes and businesses.

Each village on Hatteras has a restaurant or two that are listed below. You may want to call to make sure they are open during the off-season. Many close after Thanksgiving and reopen during late spring.

Don't Miss

Drinks and appetizers at Rusty's
Apple Uglies at Orange Blossom
Fish specials at Ketch 55

Sushi at Diamond Shoals
Hatteras Flat at Cafe 12
Crab cakes at the Fish House
Frozen custard at Uncle Eddy's

Foodie Faves

Atlantic Coast Cafe, 25150 NC 12 Hwy., (across from the KOA campground), Waves, NC 27982; (252) 987-1200; atlanticcoastcafe .com; Seafood/Burgers/Breakfast; $–$$. Both locations of "ACC" are as beach casual as the menus they offer. Members of the Outer Banks Catch, they source some seafood locally for their lightly grilled wraps, seafood pasta, and fresh catch entrees. This is a nice spot to catch a late breakfast (between 11 and 1), lunch, or an inexpensive dinner. Fans swear by the fish tacos, Reuben sandwiches, and disco fries that come with cheese and gravy. **Additional location:** in Avon, 41001 NC 12 Hwy. at the Avon Pier, (252) 995-7700.

Boardwok South, 26006 NC 12 Hwy., MP 41.5, (in St. Waves Plaza), Waves, NC 27982; (252) 987-1080; boardwoksouth.com; Asian Fusion/Seafood; $$. Asian fusion meets coastal Carolina at this little no-frills eatery, a member of Outer Banks Catch. Choose between a crab soup that's creamy or Maryland-style with crab and veggies in a tomato broth. Seafood stir-fry, shrimp and crab lo mein, or tempura shrimp are tempting entrees. Other diners rave about the grilled crab cakes. A few beers are on tap, or try some sake. And who wouldn't want to try the chocolate egg rolls? A take-out menu is available.

Cafe Pamlico, 49684 NC 12 Hwy., at the Inn at Pamlico Sound, Buxton, NC 27920; (252) 995-7030; innonpamlicosound.com/Cafe Pamlico; Seafood/American; $$$–$$$$. Hatteras Island finally has a fine-dining establishment, Cafe Pamlico, located in the equally elegant Inn at Pamlico Sound. The sleek and tranquil Cafe features colorful works by local artists, and seats lining the windows that overlook the water from which your dinner may have been caught. Or, weather permitting, you may enjoy eating alfresco on the deck, or perhaps at the gorgeous copper counter in the separate bar. Chef Forrest Paddock has cooked around Hatteras for several years, and has finally found a home and his mark. His menu is seasonal, driven by locally sourced seafood, and herbs and produce from his garden. Entrees may include blue crab ravioli with wild mushrooms, or mahimahi served over Carolina Gold rice from the Charleston area, or in a nod to the area's hunting history, a pan-roasted duck breast with chanterelles and arugula. An Outer Banks favorite, jumbo lump crab cakes, are served with chive whipped potatoes, a sweet corn succotash, and a lemon horseradish aioli. And you may be tempted still with desserts that may include key lime pie, a local favorite, or chess pie with berries, a Southern tradition. Service is friendly and smooth, as one might expect at a high-end restaurant. The inn is a popular wedding destination site, and has a following with locals, too. So reservations are a must.

Cafe 12, 41934 NC 12 Hwy. (in the Food Lion Plaza), Avon, NC 27915; (252) 995-3602; Seafood/Burgers/Pizza; $$. A very casual, kid-friendly, small place in the corner of a strip mall, Cafe 12 provides some good food at a decent price. Hands down, you must have a "Hatteras Flat." A huge tortilla is topped with cheese that floats all over the edges, and other toppings, such a spinach and bacon, or tuna and roasted red peppers, or shrimp are added, and it arrives warm and crisp. Others love the mahi fish tacos, or the Thai chicken wrap. Dinner ends early, and specials like mahi topped with sautéed crabmeat will delight without breaking the bank.

Captain's Table, 47048 NC 12 Hwy., MP 61, Buxton, NC 27920; (252) 995-3117; Seafood; $$. I was in the mood for some fresh NC flounder, but my waitress explained there was a temporary state ban on catching them for that period of time in order to help increase their number. And since the Captain's Table serves only wild-caught, local seafood, I was out of luck. Next time, when there are no restrictions, I'll hope the whole fried flounder that comes with its back scored like a tic-tac-toe board is available. Crisp and flavorful, it's delicious. Shrimp burgers, wraps, and buffalo wings offer lighter fare, and at dinner, there's the usual fried shrimp and scal-

lops, or try the daily special, which just might include Seafood Diablo, a combination of shrimp and scallops sautéed in butter with fresh tomatoes and jalapeños, served over pasta. The large dining room

What's the Big Deal about the Gulf Stream?

Local charter boat captains refer to the Gulf Stream as the Yellow Brick Road, because of the tangle of golden seaweed, like sargasso, that clumps up in this fast-moving stream that flows northward from the Gulf of Mexico, up along the East Coast toward Canada, then hooks over toward Europe. It's warm water, and it's a powerful current. Fishermen claim you can be in shirtsleeves during the winter when they're jigging over the reefs that are fed by these tropical-like waters where wahoo, grouper, and dolphinfish (mahimahi) like to hang out. And it only takes about 45 minutes to reach the Gulf Stream from Oregon Inlet on a calm day. That's where charter boat captains like to take their paying customers, because it's almost guaranteed that they'll catch something good to eat that's also fun to catch. And commercial fishermen haul in nice fish for Outer Banks markets and restaurants, too.

reminds me of an old beach cottage with its maps and photos, and there's lots of room for families and large parties.

Capt'n Rolo's Raw Bar, 53060 NC 12 Hwy., Frisco, 27936; (252) 995-3663; Seafood; $–$$. Folks like that Capt'n Rolo's serves food later in the evening than most Hatteras restaurants, and give thumbs up to the Cajun tuna sandwich, fish tacos, and fried catch of the day. Try the fresh oysters on the half shell or steamed shrimp.

The atmosphere in this raw bar can get a bit lively with the late night crowd, so take the kids earlier in the evening, when they've got their own menu. You can bet on finding cold beer and cocktails. Happy hour is daily from 3 to 5 p.m., and there's live music late on weekend nights.

Diamond Shoals, 48042 NC 12 Hwy., Buxton, NC 27920; (252) 995-5217; diamondshoals.net; Seafood; $$–$$$. You don't come here for the atmosphere, as this is just a plain and straightforward place at the beach, near the Cape Hatteras Lighthouse. However, with a seafood market attached, you can bet you'll find plenty of fresh seafood. At times, there are not just one but half a dozen "catches of the day" to choose from the list on the chalkboard. They've won the local seafood chowder contest several years, so be sure to try the clam chowder or the crab bisque with tomato and basil. Breaded and fried is the norm here, unless you've come for sushi, offered nightly in the lounge area, and then you'll have quite a variety of rolls, *nigiris,* and even a seaweed salad to choose from. Burgers, wraps, and fish sandwiches or baskets of fried oysters, clam strips, etc., served with homemade tartar sauce are on the lunch menu. And surfers and fishermen can start their day early with a huge breakfast, with options that include omelets, sausage biscuits, or hotcakes. On Sunday, there's a huge breakfast bar. Kids have an extensive menu of their own, and large parties can be accommodated.

Dolphin Den, 40126 NC 12 Hwy., MP 55, Kinnakeet, NC 27959; (252) 995-7717; dolphindenrestaurant.com; Seafood/Barbecue; $$–$$$. One of the owners of the Dolphin Den is the 10th generation to call Hatteras Island home. Armed with her grandmother's recipes, and with childhood friends who are commercial fishermen and crabbers, the menu is truly traditional, old Outer Banks style. The fresh seafood they obtain is what makes them shine. Don't fill up on their delicious corn bread, because you'll want to indulge in their signature she-crab soup or handmade crab cakes, both full of chunks of crabmeat. There's the usual assortment of seafood on the menu that can be fried or broiled, and some pastas, too. The pulled pork, chicken, and ribs have a great smoky flavor, as they are smoked in house, and hand-cut steaks are grilled, as are mahi, tuna, and salmon. Many rave about their key lime pie and brownies, too, so you'd better save some room for dessert. The decor is very laid-back and simple, with booths and expansive table seating that will accommodate large parties, so it can get noisy. A children's menu is available, too. The Dolphin Den also offers several take-out dinner options with sides that serve 8 to 10 people. Just order ahead for what they call "Our Meals, Your Wheels."

Fish House, 48962 NC 12 Hwy., Buxton, NC 27920; (252) 995-5151; Seafood; $–$$$. The Fish House is a very simple, unpretentious little place that sits next to the Buxton Harbor, which is actually one of the tiniest harbors in the Outer Banks, but where you can watch fishermen unload their boats. Under new management and refurbished since Hurricane Irene's flooding, it's still a bit of a hole in the wall. But go, just to try the "Fat Daddy" crab cake, a huge ball of backfin crab rolled in crushed potato chips, then deep-fried and served with a spicy pineapple salsa. This health-conscious foodie loved it. The Hatteras-style chowder was chock-full of fresh clams, too. Also homemade by the chef-owner are the colossal clam strips, served as a dinner. I do object, though, to the use of plastic plates and forks, both aesthetically for a $20 meal, and environmentally.

Good Winds, 24502 NC 12 Hwy. (Waves Village), MP 40, Rodanthe, NC 27968; (252) 987-1100; goodwindsrestaurant.com; Seafood; $$–$$$. As members of the Outer Banks Catch, Good Winds serves up generous portions of fresh-caught fish you'll find as specials and on the regular menu. Asian noodle bowls are loaded with veggies, and then topped with your choice of tuna, shrimp, or chicken. There are seafood baskets of fried shrimp or sea scallops, or burgers, tacos, and subs, as well as pizzas and salads. Some specials include prime rib, or an all-you-can-eat fish fry. Since Good Winds is up on the second floor, you get fantastic views of the Roanoke Sound and sunset, and there's lots of room for families and large parties. North Carolina craft beer, pale ales, seasonal beer from all over, and hard cider are among a large selection of brews.

Happy Belly Ice Cream, Smoothies & Candies, 57204 NC 12 Hwy., MP 71, Beacon Shops, Hatteras Village, NC 27943; (252) 995-2037; Ice Cream; $. The best thing you can buy in this ice cream shop is the cool T-shirt with the fat and happy Buddha on the front. While they do not make their own ice cream here, kids of all ages love the vast selection of toppings and the real fruit smoothies. Plus, there's fresh, locally made fudge and saltwater taffy.

Hurricane Heather's, 46948 NC 12 Hwy., Buxton, NC 27920; (252) 995-3060; Seafood/Burgers; $$. Three women, each with a long history of restaurant and/or business savvy, teamed up to open Hurricane Heather's, where the old Finnegan's used to be, opposite the turn for the Cape Hatteras Lighthouse. It's a lively place. A black and white diamond floor echoes the lighthouse, and bright paints and fun artwork give it an updated look. If you're a Pittsburgh Steeler fan, you're in luck, for Heather, a former bartender and now co-owner, makes sure the big-screen TVs in the bar are set for the games. There's live music some evenings, too. The Raw Bar serves up steamed shrimp or oysters on the half shell. There's plenty of table seating that's suitable for families and large groups. Customers rave about the buffalo chicken dip and their hush puppies, fried with a little bit of onion. Local produce and some local fish are featured. Mahimahi may be grilled and served over greens, then drizzled with a warm balsamic vinaigrette, or fried and served with a homemade tartar sauce. The pimiento bacon cheeseburger causes a meltdown with other fans. Heather's is where a lot of locals like to hang out, and you will, too.

Ketch 55 Seafood Grill, 40396 NC 12 Hwy., MP 55.5, Avon, NC 27915; (252) 995-5060; mackdaddysobx.com; Seafood/American; $$$. Ketch 55 rates among the best restaurants in the Outer Banks. Chef Seth Foutz has helped transform what was Mack Daddy's, a great seafood place, into this fine dining establishment. Flooding from Hurricane Irene required owner Jomi Price to do some remodeling, so the building was raised several feet and enjoyed a beautiful makeover. So did the menu. While the decor remains casual, there's a bit of worldly elegance thrown in that's reflected in the menu as well. Chef Foutz studied culinary arts in Ireland and has brought his youthful but sophisticated vision to the menu, using fresh, local seafood and produce in a refreshing and creative way. Modest, he claims he cooks as he would for his mother. She's a lucky woman. The sautéed crab salad is a delicious appetizer, a hot dip to smear on baguette slices, with a lemon butter sauce finished with diced tomatoes, scallions, and fried capers. Another marvelous starter is the classic French sausage with red wine, veal, and pork, served on a pita wedge and topped with pesto and Parmesan. The fresh catch, offered daily, may include sushi-grade tuna, mahimahi, or flounder, and you choose whether to grill, pan-sear, or have it blackened. The pan-roasted mahi served over orzo pasta with Gouda cheese and cherry tomatoes, surrounded by a ruby sea of a slightly sweet roasted beet vinaigrette is a delight to the eyes and palate. Another wonderful special is a fillet of John Dory, a local fish with a delicate white flesh, served with artichokes over tapenade and Parmesan risotto. The menu also includes the ubiquitous fried seafood, or Thai glazed tuna with wasabi, served here with pad thai. There are even some great beef and pork chop options. A lovely bar set in the middle offers clams, oysters, or mussels by the pound, as well as a really nice selection of wines (at a decent price), cocktails, and beer. And save yourself room for some dessert, too. The apple turnovers served with house-made cinnamon ice cream was such a treat. Waitstaff are friendly and keep things running smoothly. Reservations are not accepted, but kids are. See Chef Seth Foutz's recipe for **Scallops Carbonara** on p. 200.

Oceana's Bistro, 41008 NC 12 Hwy., Avon, NC 27915; (252) 995-4991; oceanasbistro .com; Seafood/Breakfast; $$–$$$. A casual eatery with a beach-y theme, Oceana's offers a varied breakfast menu with biscuits and gravy, french toast, quesadillas, and omelets. For lunch and dinner, the Black & Blue cheeseburger with blue cheese is a favorite, as are the "create your own" quesadillas, wraps, or stuffer potatoes. Find the daily specials on the chalkboard. Sesame-seared tuna, their signature dish, comes as an appetizer or entree; nachos served with a creamy white cheddar sauce with tuna, shrimp, and scallops are also a frequently ordered appetizer. Try the sweet potato fries, dusted with cinnamon, and save room for the coconut bomb cake. You can also sit at the bar with its large-screen TVs for a cold beer or mixed drinks, or entertain kids and groups in the larger dining area.

Open Water Grill, 39450 NC 12 Hwy., Avon, NC 27915; (252) 995-0003; openwatergrill.com; Seafood; $$-$$$. You may come here in board shorts and flip-flops, but you'll find white linen tablecloths on which the finest and freshest local produce and local seafood are served. And you'll have a terrific view of the sunset. A group of four young people have created a buzz in Avon. Hatteras Island recently voted in a new law that allows liquor by the drink. So Gene, the mixology master, is able to provide some amazing cocktails. And if you should need it, they've got a shuttle service to take you back to where you are staying. Chef Sam, who likes to catch some surf, has cooked professionally in Europe and on the west coast. The restaurant could not open until the experienced but young company president Cecily turned 21, so that she could apply for the needed ABC permit. General manager Martin helped design the restaurant concept, after working in places from Honolulu to Virginia Beach. Colorful walls, artwork, and the scene from the windows create quite an upbeat atmosphere. And the food? Daily specials feature local seafood, and only when it's in season. Steaks and chicken, and some fish fillets, are grilled over charcoal. You'll also find pasta, ribs, and "fish fry or boil pots" featuring crab, shrimp, and clams. And aren't you enticed by the "World's Ugliest Chocolate Cake," which the menu suggests you need sunglasses and a spoon to eat?

Orange Blossom Bakery & Cafe, 47208 NC 12 Hwy., Buxton, NC 27920; (252) 995-4109; orangeblossombakery.com; Baked Goods/Breakfast; $. You've got to try the Apple Uglies, these huge apple fritters filled with apple chunks and swirled with cinnamon, fried, then glazed, and as one option, covered with chocolate. Go early, before 9 a.m (it's only open between 6:30 and 11 a.m.) to ensure you get your own Apple Ugly or else order via phone. Cinnamon rolls and double-dipped doughnuts have their own following, too. Veggie breakfast burritos, bagels, breakfast sandwiches, fresh bread, cookies, and pastries are also on the menu. You'll find some good coffee, too. This bakery is in an old wooden building that used to be the Orange Blossom Motel, named for the orange trees that grew there. Even though it's right on the road, it's still easy to miss. Look for the bright blue sign in the curve after the lighthouse. There's some crowded seating indoors, and a few tables on the small porch.

Quarterdeck Restaurant, 54214 NC 12 Hwy., Frisco, NC 27936; (252) 986-2425; Seafood; $$. Members of the Outer Banks Catch, this family-owned restaurant has been serving seafood for decades. Don't expect anything fancy in this cinderblock place. The decor is simple, as is the menu. Fried or broiled seafood, Hatteras-style clam chowder, and some sandwiches are offered along with char-grilled steaks. The crab cakes have some fans, as well as the hush puppies. The catch of the day, like fresh, local bluefish, may be your best bet. Kids and large parties are welcome.

Rusty's, 47355 NC 12 Hwy., Buxton, NC 27920; (252) 995-4184; rustyssurfnturf.com; Seafood/Caribbean Fusion; $$$. **Chef-Owner**

Rusty Midgett was born and raised on Hatteras, and learned to balance life with a surfboard. That passion led him to catching waves in the Caribbean, the Mexican Riviera, and the Pacific Rim. Along the way, his day job, cooking, was influenced by the tropical flavors he encountered. After chef stints in some major Philadelphia restaurants where he had a following, he decided to return home to surf and cook. He buys his seafood straight off the boats that come into Avon's old harbor on the soundside. Shrimp and crab spring rolls, Caribbean-spiced wahoo topped with mango habañero salsa and served with pigeon peas and rice, and fish tacos with the catch of the day reflect his fusion of tropical cuisines and style with that of the Outer Banks. Other seasonal specials, like crispy roast duck in the fall, or blackened scallops with lemon rosemary aioli, and chile- and cumin-scented mahimahi over mashers and succotash, will make your taste buds happy. You'll keep going back for the duck enchiladas, a delicious appetizer. The regular menu also features "Calabash"-style fried seafood, which refers to the small coastal town near the South Carolina border where fry-houses reign, and gumbo and jambalaya, recipes he learned from his mother's family. You'll find the decor very upbeat, with bright, Caribbean colors and bold artwork. Visit Jody, the mixologist in the bar, for some fun drinks or American sipping whiskeys, now that Hatteras recently passed the liquor-by-the-drink law. It can get crowded during the summer season, so reservations are recommended.

Shipwreck Grill, 46618 NC 12 Hwy., MP 61, Buxton, NC 27920; (252) 995-5548; streammercial.com/cape/shipwreck-grill; Breakfast/Burgers; $$–$$$. Grab a seat on the large screened porch or inside at this casual, laid-back beach eatery that serves breakfast until it's time for lunch, and that lunch menu keeps rolling through dinner. Needless to say, that's popular for the crowd that likes to sleep in. You'll find the usual breakfast items, and wraps, shrimp burgers, salads, and sandwiches for lunch. Dinner features the same along with a daily special.

Uncle Eddy's Frozen Custard, 46860 NC 12 Hwy., Buxton, NC 27920; (252) 995-4059; Ice Cream; $. This is a Hatteras Island tradition for many repeat vacationers. I have it on good authority, a 10-year-old and her younger brother, that Uncle Eddy's is a real treat. She had been talking about it the whole way from Ohio, her mother said. Here they make their own frozen egg custard and offer lots of flavors you can mix, with several different sundaes available.

Waves Market & Deli, 26006 NC 12 Hwy., St. Waves Plaza, Waves, NC 27982; (252) 987-2352; Deli/Seafood; $–$$. At this cool stop that also includes shelves full of snacks, condiments, wine, and other grocery items, you'll find a terrific deli menu that includes a variety of sandwiches, along with daily specials like local shrimp and papaya quesadillas, or yellowfin tuna salad, and old-fashioned, homemade chicken and dumplings. Enjoy the variety of microbrews, too. Grab hot dogs and meats for burgers, along with garnishes and charcoal. Catch some homemade baked goods, like red velvet cake and cookies, too.

Pizza & Pasta

Angelo's Pizza, 46898 NC 12 Hwy., Buxton, NC 27920; (252) 995-6364; $$. Although it doesn't look like much from the outside, you'll find decent pizza and calzones, subs, spaghetti, and cheese steak subs here.

Gidget's Pizza and Pasta, 41934 NC 12 Hwy., Hatteras Island Plaza, Avon, NC 27915; (252) 995-3109; pizzagidget.com; $$. Used to be known as Toppers, but now is independently run. Great pizza, baked subs, and a good variety of pastas and salads, with a nice selection of beer and a few wines.

The Gingerbread House, 52175 NC 12 Hwy., Frisco, NC 27936; (252) 995-5204; $$. Okay, it's not what you'd expect. But it does serve specialty pizza with homemade crust and sauce. It's also the place to go for a very hearty breakfast with traditional breakfast fare.

Lisa's Pizzeria, 24158 NC 12 Hwy., Rodanthe, NC 27968; (252) 987-2525; lisaspizzeria.net; $$. This place had to be renovated after Irene. Offers great pizzas and delicious calzones, and even a breakfast pizza.

Nino's Pizza, 41188 Palazzolo Rd., just off NC 12 Hwy., Avon, NC 27915; (252) 995-5358; $$. This pizza joint has been on Hatteras for over 30 years serving pizza, spaghetti, pasta dishes, and subs, along with hamburgers and salads.

Papa Nino's, 47365 NC 12 Hwy., Osprey Shopping Center, Buxton, NC 27920; (252) 986-2150; $$. An offshoot of Nino's Pizza, a few more miles south, they serve the same pizza and subs, with a lunch buffet featuring pizza.

Specialty Stores, Markets & Fishmongers

Austin's South Island Seafood & Produce, 23500 NC 12 Hwy., Rodanthe, NC 27968; (252) 987-1352. Like many markets that sell fresh, local seafood in season, Austin's South Island also stocks snow and king crab legs, mussels, and even lobsters. And they've joined the fry-up with baskets and sandwiches filled with shrimp, scallops, or oysters available for takeout. Or, order steamer pots with various seafood combinations that you take and cook, or they'll steam it ahead for you.

Buxton Seafood Market, 49799 NC 12 Hwy., Buxton, NC 27920; (252) 995-5085. At this friendly family business next to the water tower, some of the fresh seafood they offer they caught themselves. You'll also find all the sauces and condiments you'll need for sushi, and they'll steam shrimp and crabs for takeout.

Diamond Shoals Seafood Market, 46843 NC 12 Hwy., Buxton, NC 27920; (252) 995-5521; diamondshoals.net/seafood-market.html.

Right beside the restaurant (see p. 142), you can catch the freshest of catches at this market to take home, or they will also fry or grill them for you. Some sides, like fries, coleslaw, and baked potatoes, are also available to go.

Island Spice & Wine, 40246 NC 12 Hwy., Avon, NC 27915; (252) 995-7750. You could spend hours browsing the over 1,000 wine labels in this delightful shop, or the microbrews from North Carolina and Virginia. Or perusing the jams, specialty sauces, and chocolates lining the shelves. A variety of special olive oils and vinegars, spices, cheese, and coffee (roasted especially for them) are also great for stocking your vacation pantry. Plus, owner Donna Haddock Hashtani carries quite an interesting variety of kitchenware and serving dishes with a coastal theme. Look for *The Outer Banks Cookbook: Recipes & Traditions from North Carolina's Barrier Islands,* Second Edition, among others.

Risky Business Seafood, 40658 NC 12 Hwy. at Kinnakeet Corner, Avon, NC 27915; (252) 995-7003; riskybseafood.com. Members of Outer Banks Catch, this market offers fresh shrimp, fish, crabs, and clams from the surrounding waters. Or they'll steam them for you to take back to your hotel or cottage to eat. Also, they will process your own catch, clean the fish, then vacuum pack it so it's ready for the freezer or stove. They make some awesome crab cakes from lump crabmeat with absolutely no filler. Try their smoked tuna, too.

St. Waves Seafood & Produce, 26006 NC 12 Hwy., Waves, NC 27982; (252) 987-2013. In the middle of the St. Waves Plaza, this delightful market not only features fresh local seafood, but will also steam shrimp for free, and stocks hand-cut Angus beef. Try Mizz Lizzie's jumbo lump crab cakes, and her famously delicious key lime pie, made in house daily. Fresh produce, when in season, is also available, as well as a full line of their private-label pickles, relishes, and jams.

Surf's Up Seafood Market, 41838 NC 12 Hwy., Avon, NC 27915; (252) 995-3432. Fresh, local seafood, of course, and with a tagline of "we kill 'em all," they will steam shrimp or pots of seafood combos for you.

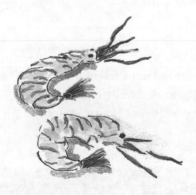

Hatteras Village

Hatteras is such a quaint fishing village. At the southernmost point of the island, it's a short ferry ride from Ocracoke Island to the south. Near the ferry terminal is the fascinating Graveyard of the Atlantic museum, and a shopping complex. But travel along its main drag that twists and turns to avoid creeks and shallow areas, and you'll find some of the oldest homes on the Outer Banks, and a thriving harbor that's home to the renowned fishing charter boat industry. There are no chain hotels or restaurants here. Folks are friendly and very laid-back. The annual Day at the Docks festival, held each September, is a must for good eating and for all the fishing stories and history.

Don't Miss

Breakfast at Sonny's
Chowder at Breakwater Restaurant
Shrimp burger at Harbor Deli
Fresh seafood at Harbor House Seafood

Foodie Faves

Billfish Bar & Grill, 58646 NC 12 Hwy., Hatteras Village, NC 27943; (252) 986-0080; teachslair.com/restaurant; Seafood/American; $$–$$$. Watch the sunset and charter boat traffic from this new eatery in an old location. Start with Pamlico clams or crab puffs, or perhaps the traditional Hatteras clam chowder or a creamy crab bisque. From the steamer you can get NC shrimp, oysters, or mussels; from the fryers, the usual variety of seafood. There are a few quesadillas, several pastas, and a few steak, chicken, and pork dishes. Kids have their own menu, too. Beer and some wine are available.

Breakwater Restaurant, 57896 NC 12 Hwy., Oden's Dock, Hatteras Village, NC 27943; (252) 986-2565; breakwaterhatteras.com; Seafood/American; $$$. Be sure to come in time to catch the sunset from the second-floor decks overlooking the Hatteras Harbor. This is a great place, a bit upscale, to celebrate the fact that you're on vacation with a wonderful companion. A member of the Outer Banks Catch, Owner Jane Oden greets you with a warm welcome to this lovely, contemporary space with tables lining windows that overlook the water. Her son Don prepares a tasty menu featuring local and seasonal seafood. Start with a "Breakwater Tini" or other cocktails, wine, or beer at the beautiful bar while you wait. Chef Don is a multiple winner of the chowder contest at the Day at  the Docks, so be sure to order whatever soups are offered, like the scallop and brie bisque, or she-crab soup. The blue crab ravioli in a creamy cheese sauce is their signature appetizer, and blackened scallops make another great starter. I've always enjoyed the daily specials featuring local catches, like a wonderful rockfish paired with crabmeat. Fresh yellowfin tuna is wrapped in a tortilla and served over black beans and rice. Or you can have a seafood medley fried or broiled. Another crowd pleaser is the filet mignon topped with lump crabmeat and a béarnaise sauce. Make sure you get a reservation, as it can be quite crowded during the season. See recipe for Sous Chef Tyler Naughton's **Black & Blue Scallops** on p. 197.

Dinky's, 57980 NC 12 Hwy. (second floor of Village Marina), Hatteras Village, NC 27943; (252) 986-2020; Seafood/American; $$$. Admire the view of the harbor and sunset and the beautiful bar and tables made from African mahogany at this small eatery. You'll probably have a wait, so sit at the bar and enjoy a martini or cocktail, or wine from a nice long list, before starting with fried goat cheese, scallops wrapped in bacon, or perhaps their blue crab ravioli. Entrees include fried or broiled seafood, seafood stew or marinara, and some chicken dishes and steaks, all served with generous portions of fresh veggies. Specials may include the grilled scallops skewered with rosemary or grouper with Parmesan. Steamed shrimp and Dungeness crab legs are available by the pound, or clams or mussels by the dozens. Thursday is sushi night, and prime rib is the special every Friday. Irish or Italian coffee is available to have with desserts, like coconut cream pie. This is not a great place for kids or large groups.

Harbor Deli, 58058 NC 12 Hwy., Hatteras Village, NC 27943; (252) 986-2500; hatterasdeli.com; Deli/Seafood; $. A great place to catch a lunch for the ferry ride over to Ocracoke, or to enjoy watching the dock while sitting on the screened porch of this second-floor deli. Members of the Outer Banks Catch, they serve fresh, local fish, breaded and fried in a sandwich, as well as a shrimp burger made by chopping up local shrimp and pressing that with breading into a patty that's grilled and served on a bun with a spicy remoulade. A Hatteras Island fish cake, made in much the same way, is good too. Be sure to get some of their delicious potato salad. Other more usual deli sandwiches, like a Reuben, are available. Fishermen can grab a breakfast sandwich or bagel and hot coffee before their day on the water.

Sonny's, 57947 NC 12 Hwy., Hatteras Village, NC 27943; (252) 986-2922; Breakfast/Seafood; $$. If you like a big breakfast, this is where you come, and you'll find local charter boat captains here before they head out for a day of fishing. Homemade biscuits, with sausage gravy if you like, or omelets or hotcakes are all delicious. For lunch, you'll find burgers, salads, and sandwiches, along with the catch of the day. If tuna is what's being caught, then you can have it grilled on a sandwich, or the freshest tuna salad ever in a lettuce wrap, or a chunk grilled as an entree for dinner. A few specials are also featured in the evening. They will even cook your catch for you, which is perfect for all those who have a successful adventure on a charter boat!

Pizza & Pasta

Rocco's Pizza, 57331 NC 12 Hwy., Hatteras Village, NC 27943; (252) 986-2150; $$. In spite of outward appearances, you can find decent pizza here with either thin or thick crust, some pasta selections, as well as steamed shrimp and crab dip.

Specialty Stores, Markets & Fishmongers

Harbor House Seafood Market, 58129 NC 12 Hwy., Hatteras Village, NC 27943; (252) 986-2039. As members of the Outer Banks Catch, the Harrison family brings you fresh tuna, wahoo, or cobia and other local fish caught by the father, Prowler, who fishes offshore, or in the sound by their son, Graham, who received a fishing boat for his 21st birthday. Mom Vicki mans the store. She'll steam shrimp or crabs, and also prepares a marvelous crab dip, crab cakes, bacon-wrapped scallops, and crab or shrimp enchiladas, ready for the oven. Fresh seafood is packed in ice for your trip. This is a super-friendly and clean business. See recipe for **Vicki's Smoked Fish Dip** on p. 183.

Lee Robinson General Store, 58372 NC 12 Hwy., Hatteras Village, NC 27943; (252) 986-2381; leerobinsongeneralstore.com. Hoop cheese and microbrews, Old Bay and homemade fudge, cookbooks and kitchenware, tackle, groceries, and just about anything else you need, including bug spray, can be found here. A great place for grabbing missing items from your pantry or snagging a great souvenir.

Risky Business Seafood, Oden's Dock (below the Breakwater Restaurant), Hatteras Village, NC 27943; (252) 986-2117; riskybseafood .com. The freshest catch is what they promise, and it's seasonal, which means some fish may not always be available. Members of the Outer Banks Catch, they'll cut fillets for you, steam shrimp and blue crab, and will pack it all for travel. They also offer custom fish cleaning, with vacuum packaging, freezing, and storing for you. Be sure to try their crab cakes, made with lump crabmeat and no filler, and their smoked tuna.

Sticky Bottom Produce, 58372 NC 12 Hwy., Hatteras Village, NC 27943; (252) 986-1037. Fresh corn, peaches, melons, and veggies like juicy sweet tomatoes and freshly dug sweet potatoes from the coastal plains of NC are found in season at this covered produce stand that's just across the road from Lee Robinson General Store.

Coffeehouse

Dancing Turtle Coffee Shop, 58079 NC 12 Hwy., Hatteras Village, NC 27943; (252) 986-4004; thedancingturtle.com; Coffee/

Pastries; $. Located in an authentic-looking Hatteras cottage, the Dancing Turtle offers a cozy and welcome place to nab a cup of java, espresso, or smoothie, or grab a baked goodie. The new co-owners are a young couple who love to kite surf, and what better place for that than Hatteras Island? Their passion for both kiting and a good cup of coffee has taken them to Brazil and other exotic spots. As a result, there are about 17 flavors and types of roasts of coffee from around the world in stock. Comfy chairs invite you to linger in the large, open space.

Ocracoke Island

Like the dot at the bottom of an exclamation point, Ocracoke Island sits at the end of a string of barrier islands and dunes. It's been called the "pearl of the Outer Banks."

When you arrive via ferry, it seems as though you've traveled to the end of the earth. From the northern ferry terminal, you travel almost 15 miles between windswept dunes and live oaks, over creeks with names like Molasses and Old Quawk's, past a pen of the wild Outer Banks ponies, with no houses or shops, just a sandy airstrip with wind funnels, until you get to the village of Ocracoke.

Ocracoke used to be the only navigable inlet on the Banks, and a treacherous port, requiring pilots to guide large vessels in. But that's what made it a good "hurricane hole," a place to escape the nasty storms that caused a great loss of ships and lives around the island. Or as in the case with Blackbeard, it was great for a pirate's hideout, at least for a while. He did lose his head here.

A large number of vessels put into port here to off-load a flow of foods, spices, spirits, and other goods from around the world, to be sent inland and up the Banks. Islanders were also good scavengers

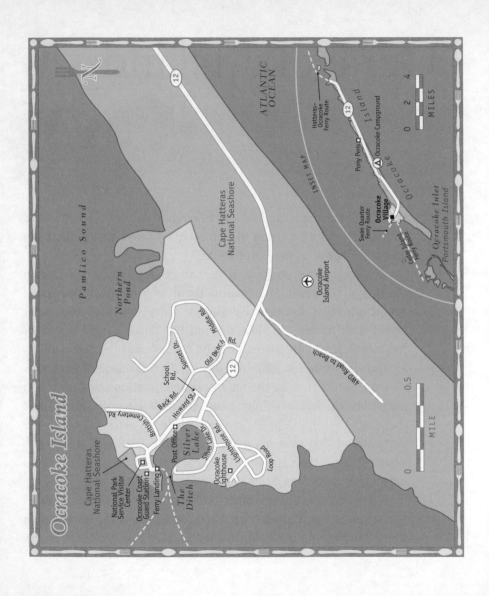

Ocracoke Island

Cape Hatteras National Seashore

National Park Service Visitor Center

Ocracoke Coast Guard Station

Ferry Landing

The Ditch

Post Office

Silver Lake

Ocracoke Lighthouse

Lighthouse Rd.

Silver Lake Rd.

Loop Road

British Cemetery Rd.

Back Rd.

School Rd.

Sunset Dr.

Middle Rd.

Howard St.

Old Beach Rd.

12

Cape Hatteras National Seashore

Northern Pond

Pamlico Sound

ATLANTIC OCEAN

Ocracoke Island Airport

4WD Road to Beach

12

INSET MAP

Hatteras-Ocracoke Ferry Route

Ocracoke Campground

Pony Pens

12

Ocracoke Island

Swan Quarter Ferry Route

Ocracoke Village

Cedar Island Ferry Route

Ocracoke Inlet

Portsmouth Island

MILES

0   2   4

0   0.5   MILE

of the many wrecks that washed ashore, retrieving exotic fruits like bananas, animals, and other food stores.

And the sea fed them well. Crabs, clams, oysters, and fish from the sounds filled their bellies. Some old-timers tended vegetable gardens that were somewhat productive despite the sandy soil. Storms and hot, humid weather tended to diminish their output, and that's why in days gone past, old-time residents waited patiently for the vegetable truck that arrived every Wednesday morning via ferry.

Today, storms still wreak havoc and cut the island off from the rest of the world when the ferry service is interrupted. You'll find O'crokers a stalwart group who can hunker down with generators, or meet up at Howard's Pub, which generators keep running.

But visiting foodies needn't worry. On Ocracoke, you'll find fresh seafood gathered that day from the Pamlico Sound or the Gulf Stream featured in creatively prepared specials at several lovely restaurants. Craving pizza or Mexican? You'll find both. There are even a couple of food trucks. And take note—about nine varieties of figs grow profusely on the island, so Ocracoke fig preserves and cakes should not be missed.

And you'll also have your choice of romantic, scenic, sports bar, or family-style restaurants. Most restaurants close either at the end of October or after Thanksgiving and reopen sometime in March. That is, if the hurricane season has been kind. To be sure, call ahead. Reservations are not always taken.

Don't Miss

Breakfast, especially traditional fish cakes or fish roe at Pony Island Coffee and local chatter at Ocracoke Coffee Co.

Cioppino, shrimp and grits, or soft-shells at Dajio's

Crab puffs, Ocracoke fig cake, or hummingbird cake at Atlantic Cafe

Ocracoke fish cake or grilled fresh fish at Jason's

Cold beer and burger while watching Silver Lake traffic at sMac Nally's

Crab beignets or small plates like ahi tuna burger at Back Porch Restaurant & Wine Bar

The daily fish specials at The Flying Melon, and sweet potato biscuits

Oysters in season at Topless Oysters

Sunset drink at Howard's Pub

Foodie Faves

Back Porch Lunchbox, 747 Irvin Garrish Hwy., Ocracoke, NC 27960; (252) 929-3651; backporchocracoke.com/Back_Porch/Lunchbox.html; Lunch; $. In a small building next to the Pony Island Motel, you can grab a bag lunch or picnic for the beach or ferry ride. Fresh sandwiches, homemade baked goods, snacks, and cold drinks are available.

Back Porch Restaurant & Wine Bar, 110 Back Rd., Ocracoke, NC 27960; (252) 928-6401; backporchocracoke.com; Seafood/American; $$$. This restaurant has been a mainstay for locals and tourists alike for decades, although new owner Daphne Bennink has added a lovely bar area since liquor by the drink was passed a few years ago. Lighter fare, like ahi tuna burgers, spicy pimiento cheese fries, *croque monsieur,* and citrus calamari are served just in the bar. On the screened, temperature-controlled porch, begin your dinner with the crab beignets, crepes stuffed with crab and cream cheese, then fried. Friendly servers will steer you toward your best bets, but go for the catch of the day, whether it's shrimp simply sautéed with garden fresh veggies, or seared yellowfin tuna with mango salsa and tomatillo cream. A dish of grits and greens featured kale in season, and was to die for. Half-portions are happily served, and duck and steak round out the menu. A variety of bar drinks are available, and the wine list offers a balance of styles and prices by the glass or bottle.

Cafe Atlantic, 1129 Irvin Garrish Hwy., Ocracoke, NC 27960; (252) 928-4861; ocracokeisland.com/cafe_atlantic.htm; Seafood/Boat-to-Table/American; $$$. A personal favorite because of its unpretentious yet modern presentations of traditional Outer Banks seafood. They serve many deliciously simple "catch of the day" dinners here, like grilled yellowfin tuna, so fresh you expect it to still wiggle. And I could fill up with just their mouthwatering appetizers, like the crab puffs stuffed with mascarpone cheese or rosemary chèvre with fig preserves, made in house. Chef-Owner Ruth Toth has always focused on fresh and local, with Southern traditions thrown in. Taste her homemade pimiento cheese with fried okra, or clams casino, those fresh bivalves plucked from the Pamlico Sound out back. Besides fresh fish grilled or fried, the menu may include scallops, shrimp stuffed with crab, or seafood kebabs, and even veal piccata and beef tenderloin. Crab cakes are full of local lump crab-meat. Be sure to save room for Ruth's homemade desserts, especially Ocracoke's famous fig cake served with homemade coffee ice cream, or hummingbird cake, or chocolate bread pudding or coconut cream pie—it will be difficult to make up your mind! There's a lovely and affordable wine list, with wines available by the glass.

Capt Puddle Duck's, (Delivery Only) Ocracoke, NC 27960; (252) 588-0107; Seafood; $$. A commercial fisherman, Fletcher O'Neal, and his wife, Heather, will deliver a steamer pot filled with Ocracoke clams, shrimp, crabs, red potatoes, corn, and andouille sausage to your motel room, campsite, or wherever you might be staying on Ocracoke that has a burner or grill available to steam the pot. Then spread newspapers on a table, push up your sleeves, and dig in, with butter, cocktail sauce, spice packets, and lemon wedges provided.

The Corner Crepe, 80-110 Back Rd., Ocracoke, NC 27960; (252) 588-2100; Breakfast; $. Daphne Bennick, owner of the Back Porch, introduced this upscale food truck that features a beloved food staple of her own French family, crepes. Opening daily at 8 a.m., it's become one of the island's favorites for breakfast, offering a great alternative to the standard fare. You can get savory crepes like the Zorba, with spinach, feta, and kalamata olives, or the Creole, full of shrimp and roasted peppers. Or let your sweet tooth prevail with the sweet crepes filled with cream cheese and fresh, seasonal fruit, like blueberries or peaches, or standards like the Rum Runner, filled with caramelized, rum-flambéed bananas with chocolate ganache. There are a few tables and chairs nearby that are in the shade.

Creekside Cafe, 621 Irvin Garrish Hwy., Ocracoke, NC 27960; (252) 929-3606; ocracokecreekside.com; Seafood/American; $$. Walk around the corner from Silver Lake to this funky screened eatery, open all day, for a great breakfast or affordable lunch and dinner. Try the delicious crepes filled with chunky homemade applesauce or the shrimp omelet to start your day. Some daily specials include a very tasty corn and crab chowder and fresh local fish, shrimp, and clams. The owners are from Pittsburgh, so you'll find "yinzer" specials, like Pittsburgh cheese steaks and fries on salads.

Dajio's, 305 Irvin Garrish Hwy., Ocracoke, NC 27960; (252) 928-7119; dajiorestaurant.com; Seafood/Boat-to-Table/American; $$–$$$$. Located in what was the old Pelican restaurant on the main road around Silver Lake, Dajio's serves breakfast, lunch, and dinner. The name stands for "Doug and Judy in Ocracoke," two Lexington, KY restaurant owners who consciously migrated here. You can choose to eat outside, nestled under live oaks in the new patio area that sometimes features live music, or inside the "shabby chic," historic old house. Breakfast offers huge, scrumptious omelets, shrimp and grits, or eggs Oscar with local lump crabmeat. A shrimp tempura wrap with spicy tomato relish makes a mouthwatering lunch, as does a shrimp salad club with fried prosciutto and green chile chutney. Seasonal specials often include tempura soft-shell crabs over jasmine rice, and yellowfin tuna served with spicy tomato and seaweed salad. Grilled shrimp with fresh blue corn nachos, manchego cheese, and homemade salsa is a favorite with locals. Cioppino, a fisherman's stew made with fresh, local fish, and crab "mac and cheese," melding rich gruyère cheese sauce with fresh jumbo lump crabmeat, are two consistent crowd pleasers. Vegetarian pasta, ribs, and tenderloin help round out the menu. Some wines are available by the glass from the balanced but short wine list. Save room for Ocracoke fig cake and other yummy desserts. See Chef Doug Eifert's recipe for **Grilled Cheese with Green Chile Chutney** on p. 187.

Eduardo's Taco Truck, 950 Irvin Garrish Hwy., Ocracoke, NC 27960; (252) 588-2313; Mexican; $. One of the two food trucks on Ocracoke, Eduardo's has quite the following, with long lines some summer days of folks who don't want to have to get out of their swimsuits. Located on the edge of the Variety Store parking lot, this taco stand offers a variety of authentic Mexican dishes prepared by Eduardo Chavez Perez, who is also the lead cook for The Back Porch restaurant. Breakfast burritos, huevos rancheros, tostadas made with chicken, pork, or shrimp, and fish ceviche of local flounder are all tasty favorites with locals and visitors. And the tacos are generously stuffed and easily downed. A few picnic tables are located in the shade of nearby trees.

Fig Tree Deli & Bakery, 1015 Irvin Garrish Hwy., Ocracoke, NC 27960; (252) 928-3481; ocracokeisland.com/fig_tree.htm; Breakfast; $. Start your day with a bagel or biscuit sandwich or muffins, cinnamon rolls, and such. And of course, they offer their take on Ocracoke fig cake, made with their own homemade fig preserves. Sandwiches, wraps, and salads are perfect for picnics on the beach or a boat ride or even to take with you on the ferry. Within the shop is Sweet Tooth, a confectionery store with lots of chocolate and other tempting goodies for kids of all ages.

Flying Melon, moving to 181 Back Rd. Spring 2013 from 804 Irvin Garrish Hwy., Ocracoke, NC 27960; (252) 928-2533; ocracokeisland

.com/flying_melon.htm; Seafood/New Orleans/American; $$–$$$$. Take note: They're open for brunch and dinner, closed Mon. Owners Michael and Paula Schramel migrated from New Orleans, and that's evident in their preparations of local seafood. Michael "does beurre blanc really well," said the young server, and that was evident with the excellent grilled local mahi—tender, fleshy chunks, served with sautéed lump crabmeat. They're known for their fried green tomatoes, served with either fried oysters or steamed shrimp with remoulade. Daily specials might include local flounder either crusted with Parmesan or minced pecans and a creole meunière sauce, or pan-seared scallops with ginger orange spinach and spaghettini. Steak au poivre, pork chops, and sandwiches round out the menu. The "dessert lady" also works as a waitress, and her New Orleans bread pudding with pears and bourbon sauce was out of this world. Ditto for the strawberry chocolate cake. There's a nice affordable and diverse wine list with some available by the glass. Brunch includes omelets, *pain perdu* (a New Orleans–style french toast), salads, and sandwiches, some using the fresh catch of the day. Be sure to check out their sweet potato biscuits.

Howard's Pub and Raw Bar, 1175 Irvin Garrish Hwy., Ocracoke, NC 27960; (252) 928-4441; howardspub.com; Seafood/Burgers; $$–$$$. The first establishment you'll encounter as you drive south into the village from the Hatteras ferry, Howard's Pub is one of those places you must visit at least once. A true pub, it has about 300 brews, mixed drinks, or wine to enjoy at the bar, in one of the three dining areas, or to take up to the upstairs Sky Deck, from which you can see the ocean on one side, the sound on the other, and a great view of the sunset. The menu includes standard pub fare from around the world, but also features daily specials that include locally caught fresh fish, like grilled or broiled mahi; Ocracoke clam chowder, full of broth and clams from the Pamlico Sound out back; not-too-breaded crab cakes; fresh local shrimp, steamed or fried; and steamed clams and oysters. While waiting, amuse yourself by looking at license plates from all over the US and collections of surfboards hanging on the walls. Satisfy your sweet tooth with homemade key lime pie or chocolate peanut butter pie. Howard's Pub is family-friendly, with kids' meals served on souvenir Frisbees.

Jason's Restaurant, Highway 12, Ocracoke, NC 27960; (252) 928-3434; jasonsocracoke.com; Seafood/American; $$. Dine inside or on the screened porch, or call ahead for take out for lunch or dinner. And remember it's closed Sunday. Owner Jason Wells uses his family background of running restaurants on Ocracoke to full advantage with this casual eatery. The fresh catch of the day, "whatever the local boys caught this morning," is simply grilled and served with tasty, seasonal veggies. Or try the Jamaican jerk shrimp or chicken, with red and green peppers and pineapple, or quesadillas, or pasta with marinara or meatballs. Locals love Sushi Night, every Tuesday from Easter through Halloween, and their pizzas.

Jolly Roger, 396 Irvin Garrish Hwy., Ocracoke, NC 27960; (252) 929-3703; ocracokeisland.com/jolly_roger.htm; Seafood/Burgers; $$. You can at least expect a great view of Silver Lake here while enjoying a cold beer, with perhaps seafood gumbo, fried coconut shrimp, or tacos made with the local catch of the day, like bluefish. There's a lively crowd at lunch and at sunset, especially when there's live music.

Pony Island Restaurant, 51 Ocean View Rd., Ocracoke, NC 27960; (252) 928-4411; ocracokeisland.com/pony_island.htm; Seafood/Breakfast; $$–$$$. This is one of the best places on Ocracoke for breakfast. Hope that they'll have the fish cakes, made by the owner's mother, Peggy O'Neal, with whatever's the local catch—be it bluefish or an island favorite, drum—mixed with boiled potatoes, then hand-fashioned and fried. The other local specialty offered in season is fish roe, fried and served with scrambled eggs. Folks rave about the Pony Potatoes, hash browns with melted cheese, salsa, and sour cream. Hotcakes and biscuits, sausage, and bacon with eggs round out the usual Southern breakfast fare. Dinner appetizers feature Ocracoke crab balls, and a pizza topped with lump crabmeat and veggies. Entree favorites include crab cakes from a family recipe, and the usual seafood assortments served either fried or broiled. The interior is no-frills, but the service is gracious, and it's very family-friendly.

FIGS ON THE OUTER BANKS

Walk the quiet back roads of the villages of Ocracoke or Hatteras, and you will see at least one large fig tree in a sunny, wind-protected spot, with an array of oyster or clam shells around its base. Figs grow profusely in this humid, salty air, and there's a legend that once the original owners move from a house, its fig tree will die from mourning. Actually, it's probably being neglected since the shrub needs regular doses of nutrients, be it from the lime leeched from the oyster shells, or perhaps from the leftover pot liquor that used to be thrown on its roots.

Nine varieties of figs are grown on Ocracoke alone, with names like Celeste (also known as Sugar), Blue, Brown Turkey, and Pound, so named for how much it weighs. Wasps and birds have to be shooed away from the ripening fruit, and the fruit is so tender, it doesn't last long once picked. Ladies on the Outer Banks traditionally preserved the harvest of figs as, well, preserves. If you see any jars of Ocracoke fig preserves for sale, get them. On toast, or on goat cheese and crackers, it's divine.

Fig preserves are used to make the famous Ocracoke Fig Cake, a moist nut-filled batter with cinnamon, cloves, nutmeg, and allspice that only gets better after sitting for a day or two, if you can keep the nibblers away. Ladies on Ocracoke have a bit of a competitive spirit, some boasting that their slight variation is better than others. On Hatteras, a spirited version is popular, one that calls for a bit of whiskey in the recipe. Be sure to try this marvelous traditional dessert, either frosted with cream cheese, or served with ice cream, or just by itself.

sMac Nally's, 180 Irvin Garrish Hwy., Ocracoke, NC 27960; (252) 929-9999; smacnallys.com; Seafood/Burgers; $$. Located right at the Anchorage Inn Marina on Silver Lake, you can't beat the view of sunset here. Locals claim sMac Nally's has the best cheeseburger, made with a half pound of Angus beef and served with crispy curly fries. I've enjoyed a great soft-shell sandwich when those crabs are in season. Peel 'n eat shrimp and fish-and-chips are also good. It's a terrific place to enjoy a cold beer and a bite to eat while checking out visiting sailors and recreational fishermen.

Thai Moon, 158 Irvin Garrish Hwy., in Spencer's Markets, Ocracoke, NC 27960; (252) 928-5100; Thai; $. Offering takeout only, Thai Moon might give you a break from the island's seafood theme. Some find delightful the chicken satay, pad thai with shrimp or chicken, ginger flounder, crab rice, and other traditional Thai dishes made with local seafood that's cooked by Moon, a transplant from Thailand who has been on the island for years. Note that it's cash only.

Topless Oyster, 875 Irvin Garrish Hwy., Ocracoke, NC 27960; (252) 928-2800; toplessoyster.com; Seafood; $$. Steamed, fried, or ceviche-style, oysters are served in a variety of ways in this new eatery opened by a couple who longed to return to the island after the Gulf oil spill closed their first restaurant. Oyster Po'Boys lead the way among other seafood sandwiches, along with North Carolina barbecue. Entrees also include stuffed shrimp, rib eyes, pasta, and fried seafood platters. Open for lunch and dinner, it's family-friendly.

Specialty Stores, Markets & Fishmongers

La Isla Mexican Grocery, 588 Irvin Garrish Hwy., in Spencer's Market, Ocracoke, NC 27960; (252) 928-2626. An interesting market for the growing number of Hispanic residents of Ocracoke that also provides some shopping diversity for the tourist, La Isla offers avocados, tomatillos, dried beans and chiles, fresh cheeses, mole pastes, Mexican spices, and some fresh veggies. The owners bring freshly made corn tortillas from their own factory and fresh breads and sweets from an uncle's bakery, located across the sound in Washington, NC.

Ocracoke Seafood Market, 294 Irvin Garrish Hwy., Ocracoke, NC 27960; (252) 928-5601; ocracokeisland.com/ocracoke_seafood.htm. The very last of the many fish houses that used to line Silver Lake, the Ocracoke Seafood Market only sells what's brought in by local fishermen who unload their catch on the dock out back. It's also the heart and home of the Ocracoke Working Watermen's Association, a marvelous organization dedicated to preserving the heritage and future of local, working fishermen. Look for briny fresh clams from ClamLady Jane, live blue crabs, oysters, shrimp, tuna, flounder, and other fish plucked from the waters surrounding the island. You can also get steamed shrimp or crab. Supporting this group is highly recommened, so purchase fresh seafood here for your cottage kitchens or to take back home.

Ocracoke Variety Store, 950 Irvin Garrish Hwy., Ocracoke, NC 27960; (252) 928-4911; ocracokevarietystore.com. "If we don't have it, you probably don't need it," says the owner. And true, you can find regular grocery items, hardware, ice, fishing supplies, and freshly cut meats here. There's also a surprisingly nice selection of wine, and of course, beer.

Zillie's Pantry, 538 Back Rd., Ocracoke, NC 27960; (252) 929-9036; zilliespantry.com. This upscale store offers over 300 craft beers, eight brews on tap, and bottles of wine from around the world, as well as some other good provisions, like a variety of upscale cheeses, salami, prosciutto, and the crackers to go with them, along with packaged cookies and candies. There's also quite a bit of kitchenware to peruse, and kitschy local posters. Every Thursday at 6 p.m. you can sample five wines paired with light hors d'oeuvres, reservations only. Or anytime they're open, just get a brew or wine by the glass, some snacks, and enjoy the huge "wine and Wi-Fi" front porch.

Coffeehouses

Live Oak Coffee, 271 Irvin Garrish Hwy., Ocracoke, NC 27960; (252) 928-0115; liveoakcoffeeorcracoke.com; $. Located in an old house on the edge of Silver Lake across from the Community Square, this coffee house is run by a young trio who are dedicated to "brew with intention." Asked what they meant by that, they said that each cup of coffee comes with a conscience—knowing who the growers are, their story, and the microroasters as well. I loved the single-origin, pour-over by the cup; espressos and drip coffees are also available, as well as iced lattes. Comfortable seating invites you to play checkers, enjoy Wi-Fi, or the Zen-like quotes written on the walls. Fresh muffins, bagels, and bananas are available, too, along with cold drinks.

Ocracoke Coffee Company, 226 Back Rd., Ocracoke, NC 27960; (252) 928-7473; ocracokecoffee.com; $. If you want to know what's going on in Ocracoke, hang out with the locals who gather on the front porch of Ocracoke Coffee Co. every morning. Some days you have to wait in a long line to order different roasts of Fair Trade and/or Rainforest Alliance certified coffee, freshly ground, or a double-shot espresso, or one of their many lattes. Huge, gooey cinnamon buns, scones, and muffins are baked fresh every day. Hunker down on comfy sofas and chairs inside this old house, or claim a chair outside under the shade of huge live oaks, or even in a swing. If you like the coffee, you can take home a bag of beans or order them online. It's also one of the few places on Ocracoke with free Wi-Fi.

Recipes

If you're a good cook, and love seafood, you can't help but be inspired by all the marvelous seafood plucked from the waters surrounding the Outer Banks. For a reminder of the great tastes you've encountered here, find a good seafood market in your area, and get to know the staff, who will provide you with the freshest local products available. Then check out the recipes shared here by some great professional chefs at prominent restaurants up and down "the Banks," as well as from a seafood market owner who loves to tell you how to prepare the great seafood she stocks, and from my own stash of tried-and-true family favorites. For even more recipes, see my regional cookbook, *The Outer Banks Cookbook: Recipes & Traditions from North Carolina's Barrier Islands* (Second Edition, 2013), also by Globe Pequot Press.

Vicki's Smoked Fish Dip

For some of the freshest seafood on Hatteras Island, stop at the pretty, cottage-like Harbor House Seafood Market in the bend of the road across from the Hatteras Harbor Marina, close to the ferry dock. There, Vicki Harrison will tempt you with seafood brought in fresh by the men in her life—her husband and son, each on his own boat. Buy it fresh to take home and cook, or Vicki will steam shellfish, make oven-ready seafood dishes, or have fresh deli salads and crab dip ready to go.

Vicki shared this recipe for a marvelous, tasty smoked fish dip. She likes to use local fish that's been smoked, like bluefish, king mackerel, or speckled trout, but says that smoked salmon works as well. "Salad fishes"—tilefish, cobia, wahoo, red drum, or mahimahi—are what she likes to poach. Enjoy this dip either hot or cold, on crackers or toasted baguettes. "Ritz crackers are really better than any of the fancier crackers," says Vicki.

Yield: About 2 cups

½ pound fish fillets (tilefish, cobia, wahoo, red drum, or mahimahi)

8 ounces cream cheese, softened

½ cup mayonnaise

¼ teaspoon bottled horseradish

2 teaspoons Texas Pete hot sauce

2 splashes Worcestershire sauce

2 pinches garlic powder

2 pinches cayenne pepper

½ pound smoked fish, dark blood line and skin removed, and chopped fine

Poach the fish first, so that it can cool down while you continue with the rest of the recipe. Remove the dark blood line and skin of the fish fillet and cut the fish into chunks. In a large sauté pan, over high heat, bring a couple of inches of water to a boil. Add chunks of the fish fillet, cover with a lid, and turn the heat down to medium low. Cook for about 4 to 5 minutes, or until the fish is just tender and slightly pink. Do not overpoach or it will get too tough. Take the fish out of the water and it will continue to cook while it cools.

Mix together the remaining ingredients, except for the smoked fish, until smooth. Add all of the fish, poached and smoked, and mix well. You may heat in the microwave if you'd like to serve the dip hot, or refrigerate until needed.

Serve the dip hot or cold, preferably with Ritz crackers.

Courtesy of Vicki Harrison at the Harbor House Seafood Market (p. 160)

Inauthentic OBX Clam Chowder

A big bowl of clam chowder is an excellent reminder of one's love for the Outer Banks. This recipe is a riff on the authentic Hatteras Island chowder (see the traditional recipe in The Outer Banks Cookbook: Recipes & Traditions from North Carolina's Barrier Islands, Second Edition). *Natives would scoff at the addition of carrots and tomatoes, but would give a nod of approval to the use of bacon or country ham and the lack of cream or milk! If you cannot find minced clams at your seafood market, look for them in the freezer section of your grocery, or canned clams will do. Remember to taste the broth before adding salt, because clams and broth can be naturally rather salty.*

Yield: 4 to 6 servings

1 pint minced clams, or 2 to 3 cans chopped clams, with juice (usually they are in 6½- or 10-ounce cans)

2 slices thick bacon, fat cut away and finely chopped (scissors work best), or ¼ cup minced country ham

1 medium yellow onion, finely chopped

2 (8-ounce) bottles clam juice

2 cups water

1 (14-ounce) can diced tomatoes

3 cups diced red or white potatoes, with skins

½ cup diced carrots

Salt to taste

½ teaspoon black pepper, freshly ground

2 teaspoons Old Bay seasoning, or to taste

2 tablespoons chopped fresh parsley

Drain the clams and reserve the juice.

Place chopped bacon in a large, heavy-bottom pot, then turn heat to medium high. When bacon begins to sizzle, add the onion, and lower heat to medium low. (If using country ham, add about one tablespoon of oil to the pan, then cook the ham and onions together.) Stir frequently, and cook until onions are just tender and translucent.

Add the bottled clam juice plus the juice from the minced clams, water, tomatoes, potatoes, and carrots to the pot. Turn the heat to medium high, and bring mixture to a boil, then lower heat to a simmer and cook until potatoes are tender, about 20 to 25 minutes.

Taste the broth and add salt to taste, the pepper, and Old Bay. Add the minced clams and simmer for another 10 minutes, until clams are heated through and fairly tender.

Taste the chowder for seasoning and add chopped parsley. Stir, then serve in large bowls.

Courtesy of Elizabeth Wiegand

Grilled Cheese with Green Chile Chutney

Dajio's adds such lovely options to the dining scene on Ocracoke Island. I love sitting on the new brick terrace on sunny, cooler days for lunch or for a beer and steamed shrimp late in the afternoon, and the candlelit interior of the old former home sets the stage for a romantic dinner. Dajio stands for "Doug and Judy in Ocracoke," the culmination of a dream for this former Kentucky couple who ran a restaurant there. Chef/co-owner Doug Eifert is a staunch supporter of local and sustainable seafood, and his menu includes offerings from the waters surrounding Ocracoke Island.

This grilled cheese sandwich is one of their top sellers, says Chef Eifert. Note that the green chile chutney must be prepared first, but it can be stored in the refrigerator for future use, too. You can use any combination of mild to hot fresh chiles, he says, and substitute other types of sweeteners, like maple syrup or agave nectar, for the sugar. And use different types of cheese, if you like, but make sure they are complementary. He likes to combine nutty and earthy cheeses to balance the sweet-hot chutney.

A panini press would work well for this sandwich, also.

Yield: 1 sandwich

For the Green Chile Chutney

2 cups chopped green chiles that have been fire-roasted, seeded, and peeled

1 jalapeño, fire-roasted, seeded, peeled, and chopped

½ cup sugar

¼ cup apple cider vinegar

1 teaspoon chopped fresh thyme (if using dried, just a pinch)

1 teaspoon chopped fresh oregano (if using dried, just a pinch)

For Each Grilled Cheese Sandwich

1 tablespoon butter, or more as needed

2 slices country white bread or a buttery homemade brioche

3 ounces sliced manchego cheese

3 ounces quality farmhouse cheddar, cut into thin slices

2 heaping tablespoons green chile chutney

3 slices cooked thick-cut cherry-smoked bacon

To make green chile chutney, in a heavy-bottom saucepan, combine all ingredients. Over medium heat, bring just to a boil. Reduce heat, then cook, stirring occasionally, until it reaches a syrup-like consistency, about 10 minutes. Cool, then refrigerate until needed.

Place the butter in a skillet (preferably cast iron), then heat the pan over medium heat until butter has melted. Place the bread in the skillet, then the cheese on top of the bread. Put the chutney on top of the cheese (not directly on the bread, or it would get mushy). Then put the bacon on top of each slice.

Cook to a golden brown, making sure the cheese is fully melted. Then press the two pieces together, and serve immediately.

Courtesy of Doug Eifert at Dajio's (p. 170)

Steamed Clams with Pasta

Steaming fresh clams, then serving them with their broth over pasta, makes an easy and hearty dish. A variation of this basic recipe that my family enjoys is to include bits of country ham or cooked bacon, complemented with smoked paprika. Try dipping slices of a baguette into the broth once the clams are gone!

Yield: 2 to 4 servings

2 to 4 dozen fresh clams

1 to 2 tablespoons olive oil

1 small onion, chopped

2 cloves garlic, minced

1 (14-ounce) can diced tomatoes

½ to 1 teaspoon smoked paprika

Optional: 2 slices bacon, chopped or ¼ cup chopped country ham

2 tablespoons chopped fresh parsley

1 pound linguine or angel hair pasta, cooked

Scrub clams under cold water with a brush to remove any sand. Discard any that are open or cracked. (Do not wash until you're ready to cook, as fresh water kills the clams.) Set clams aside.

In a large pot that has a fitted lid, heat the olive oil over medium heat. Add the onion and bacon, if using. Sauté until the onions are soft. Add the garlic and stir for just a minute.

Drain just a bit of the liquid from the can of tomatoes, then add the chopped tomatoes and paprika to the pot. If using country ham, add at this point. Stir and cook for about 2 to 3 minutes, until the mixture comes to a soft boil.

Add the cleaned clams. Place the lid on the pot, and let the clams cook for about 5 minutes. Check to see if the clams are opening, and remove pot from heat as soon as they are all open, which may take about 5 minutes longer. If you have some that are stubbornly refusing to open, remove the open ones, and allow the closed ones to steam more. Then, when you are ready to serve, stir the opened clams back into the sauce to warm them up. Discard any clams that fail to open.

Place hot pasta for each serving in a shallow bowl, and place opened clams on top. Spoon cooking liquid over all. Sprinkle with the chopped parsley. Serve immediately.

Courtesy of Elizabeth Wiegand

Pan-Seared Fresh Red Drum
with Shrimp & Arugula

At the Basnight's Lone Cedar Cafe on the causeway to Nags Head, the menu features the name of the local fisherman who caught each of the day's fish specials. That's how committed they are to serving only local seafood. Chef Bud Gruninger also prefers the local green-tail shrimp that are hauled in during late fall, and freezes a bevy to be used until the spring shrimp find their way to local docks.

Red drum is a fish highly prized by Outer Bankers. Big drum catches are legendary and used to feed whole villages. You'll find smaller red drum fillets in the markets that make a tasty meal for sure. This is a fairly simple but totally awesome dish—pretty and delicious!

Yield. 4 servings

For the Fish

2 pounds fresh Outer Banks red drum fillets, skin removed

Salt and pepper to taste
1 ounce olive oil

Heat a large sauté pan over high heat. Meanwhile, sprinkle the fish fillets with salt and pepper. Add the olive oil, and when it is very hot, place the fish in the pan, and sear on one side until it's two-thirds done. Flip the fish over to brown the other side, until fish is just barely cooked through. Set pan aside.

For the Sauce

4 tablespoons butter

1 pound green-tail shrimp,
  peeled and deveined

1 large fresh tomato, diced

1 clove garlic, minced

4 cups fresh arugula

¼ cup white wine

Salt and pepper to taste

Head a sauté pan over medium high heat. Add butter and shrimp and sauté for 2 minutes, until shrimp are just barely pink all the way through.

Add tomato, garlic, arugula, white wine, and salt and pepper. Toss about for about 1 minute to heat all.

To Assemble the Dish

Remove the fish from the pan onto a cutting board. Divide into four pieces and place on four plates, prettiest side up. Top with the shrimp and veggie mix. Serve immediately.

Courtesy of Chef Bud Gruninger at Basnight's Lone Cedar Cafe (p. 102)

Sanderling Crab Cakes

Crab cakes are among my very favorite treats from the Outer Banks, but I prefer them with very little filler and just a touch of seasoning, to allow the marvelous taste of the crab to shine. The Sanderling Resort's Executive Chef Jeffrey Russell shared this classic, Outer Banks–style crab cake, done just right.

Note that many Southern chefs and cooks prefer the Dukes brand of mayonnaise. And here's a tip: I have better success with crab cakes holding together while cooking if they have been refrigerated, after you form the patties, for about an hour.

The Sanderling near Duck is the Outer Banks' only AAA Four Diamond resort. In the spring of 2013, the new Kimbull's Kitchen will open at their former Left Bank restaurant. A signature steak and seafood restaurant, it will also feature a raw bar with a particularly extensive oyster selection, plus a comprehensive wine list.

Yield: 6 to 8 servings

1 pound lump crabmeat, picked free of shells and cartilage
½ cup fresh white bread crumbs
¼ cup finely chopped chives
¼ cup Dukes mayonnaise
1 egg
1 tablespoon Dijon mustard

½ lemon, juiced
¼ teaspoon Old Bay seasoning
1 teaspoon salt
Dash of cayenne pepper
All-purpose flour, for dusting
½ cup canola oil for cooking

In a large bowl, mix together all the ingredients except for the flour and canola oil. Shape into about 6 to 8 patties and dust them on both sides with flour.

In a large skillet, heat oil over medium heat. When oil is hot, carefully add the crab cakes, in batches if needed. Fry until golden brown on the first side, about 4 to 5 minutes. Carefully flip the crab cakes over and fry on the other side until also golden brown, another 4 minutes. Serve warm.

Courtesy of Executive Chef Jeffrey Russell at The Sanderling Resort (p. 56).

Oysters Rock-Yer-Fella

Amy Huggins Gaw, aka The Outer Banks Epicurean, truly believes in eating local and organically raised foods. That's what drives her menus, whether for weekly dinners, personal chef services, cooking classes, corporate training and retreats, or wedding catering. And she loves to show off the region's unique culinary resources, whether it's paddling kayaks in the sounds to visit crab shedders or taking a traditional recipe, such as oysters Rockefeller, and making it Outer Banks–style. She's also the driving force behind Outer Banks SeaSalt. Note a food processor makes for quick prep work before roasting the oysters.

Yield: 24 oysters (appetizers for 6 to 8, more or less!)

For the Hollandaise Sauce

2 egg yolks, room temperature

1 to 2 tablespoons lemon juice

½ cup melted butter, still warm, not hot

Dash of salt, white pepper, and cayenne, to taste

Place the egg yolks and half of the lemon juice in a food processor. Begin to process, and very slowly drizzle enough warm butter to reach a creamy consistency. (It usually takes all of the butter.) Add more of the remaining lemon juice to thin, if necessary. Season with salt, pepper, and cayenne.

For the Rock-Yer-Fella

1 cup frozen chopped spinach that's been thawed and drained

1 shallot

2 ounces (⅛ pound) country ham, cut into small chunks

¼ cup white wine

Dash of celery salt

1 grind of white pepper

For the Oysters and to Finish

Rock salt

2 dozen cleaned, shucked, briny oysters on the half shell

1 batch Rock-Yer-Fella

1 recipe hollandaise sauce

To prepare the Rock-Yer-Fella, mix all ingredients in a food processor until everything is chopped fine.

Preheat broiler.

On a large, lipped baking sheet, spread a thick layer of rock salt. Nestle oysters, in their shells, in the bed of salt so that they are rather level.

Top each oyster with a teaspoon of the Rock-Yer-Fella mixture, and a drizzle of the hollandaise sauce.

Broil oysters for 2 to 3 minutes, until they are bubbling and steaming, and the tops are browned. Drizzle with more hollandaise, and serve immediately.

Courtesy of Amy Huggins Gaw, aka the Outer Banks Epicurean (p. 29 & p. 61)

Black & Blue Scallops

Breakwater Restaurant overlooks the Hatteras Harbor, and provides a lovely view of the sunset, as well as the comings and goings of the charter fishing boats. Here, I've always enjoyed dinners of seasonal fresh fish, perhaps cleaned below at Oden's Dock before being brought up to the kitchen. Jane Oden oversees the front of the house while son Don takes charge of the kitchen. This recipe comes from Tyler Naughton, a young and dedicated sous chef who prepares this menu favorite. Tyler's recipe makes a generous amount and could be divided to serve as many as a dozen for a mini first course.

This recipe may seem involved, but it's fairly easy. First, you must make the white wine cream so that it's ready to be incorporated into the blue cheese sauce with spinach. Then it's just a matter of having all the ingredients ready to go, or as the French say, mise en place. *Scallops are blackened over high heat, preferably in a cast-iron skillet, then placed over a bed of angel hair pasta and topped with the lovely sauce.*

Yield: 4 to 6 main servings or 8 to 12 appetizers

White Wine Cream

1 ½ teaspoon concentrated chicken stock (e.g., Knorr's Homestyle Stock)

⅓ cup dry white wine

3 cups heavy cream

1 teaspoon cornstarch

In a heavy-bottom medium pot, dissolve the chicken base in the white wine over medium high heat, about 2 minutes. Add the heavy cream to the mixture and give it a good stir. Set aside about ¼ cup of this mixture and combine it with the cornstarch to make a slurry, or thickener.

Meanwhile, allow the cream mixture to remain on medium high heat. Do not stir. Watch it carefully, as the cream will jump to a bubbling, rapid rise. When it rises to the very top, quickly remove the cream from the heat without allowing it to boil over.

Once the cream begins to settle, set the cream back on low heat, and whisk in the cornstarch slurry, stirring for just a minute or two until the cream is thickened.

Remove from heat and set aside or refrigerate until needed.

For the Black & Blue Scallops

- 1 cup olive oil
- 1 tablespoon seafood or steak blackening seasoning
- 2 pounds scallops
- 4 tablespoons unsalted butter
- 4 teaspoons minced garlic
- 4 teaspoons minced shallot
- 3 cups white wine cream
- 16 ounces (1 pound) blue cheese, crumbled
- Salt and freshly ground pepper to taste
- 8 ounces fresh spinach
- 1 pound dried angel hair pasta, cooked

Bring a large pot of water to a simmer that you will use to reheat the pasta.

In a large bowl, mix together the olive oil and blackening seasoning, then add the scallops, turning them over several times in the seasoned oil to coat them. Allow the scallops to marinate at room temperature while you prepare the rest of the recipe.

In a large sauté pan, melt the butter over medium high heat. Add the garlic and shallots and stir until translucent and aromatic, taking care that they do not brown. Add the white wine cream and bring to a slight boil. Add the blue cheese, turn the heat down to medium, and continue to cook, stirring often, until the *cheese is melted and the sauce is thick. Turn the heat down to the very lowest, just to keep the sauce warm. Taste, and then season the sauce with salt and pepper. Fold in the spinach, which should soften but not turn into mush.*

Meanwhile, heat the cast-iron skillet (or heavy-bottom sauté pan) over high heat. When the pan is very hot, remove the scallops from the oil and drop them one by one into the heated pan. Do not allow them to touch each other. Sear the scallops on both sides until dark golden brown, removing them from the skillet to a separate plate as soon as they are "blackened" on both sides. They should be just barely cooked in the middle.

Quickly assemble the dish by first immersing the cooked pasta into the simmering water for about 30 seconds to heat it up. Drain, then place a bed of pasta on each of four to six plates. Divide the scallops evenly and place on top of the pasta. Spoon the blue cheese and spinach sauce over the scallops and pasta. Serve immediately.

Courtesy of Tyler Naughton at Breakwater Restaurant (p. 157)

Scallops Carbonara

Ketch 55, in Avon, is the old Mack Daddy's restaurant, still owned by Jomi Price, that underwent a transformation after being flooded in a series of storms and hurricanes. Besides a raised foundation and a gorgeous new interior, there's a new chef, Seth Foutz, who has also raised the bar for the menu. You'll find tasty, innovative, and traditional preparations of locally caught fish, shrimp, clams, and oysters. I love his creative spark.

Scallops carbonara with bacon is an Americanized version of a traditional Italian recipe not often seen on Outer Banks menus. It's a fairly simple recipe. Just make sure you don't overcook the scallops, for they can become rubbery. This makes a generous serving for two, or a lighter dish for four.

Yield: 2 to 4 servings

2 slices smoked bacon, diced
¼ yellow onion, diced
1 pound dry-pack scallops
1 tablespoon minced garlic
¼ cup white wine
1½ cups heavy cream
½ cup freshly grated Parmesan cheese

⅓ cup sweet peas (frozen or fresh)
4 ounces per person dried angel hair pasta, barely cooked (al dente)
1 egg
Salt and pepper to taste

In a large sauté pan, cook bacon over medium high heat until crispy. Add onion and cook until translucent.

Add scallops and garlic, and sear scallops until golden brown. This should take only about 2 to 3 minutes per side. Remove scallops from pan and set aside.

Add the white wine to the hot pan and deglaze by stirring up all the bits and pieces. When almost dry, add the heavy cream, ½ cup Parmesan cheese, sweet peas, and the cooked pasta. Bring to a boil.

Crack the egg over the top, and stir constantly to incorporate the egg and not scramble. Once thickened, add salt and pepper to taste. Add the scallops for just a minute to allow them to reheat.

Divide evenly among dinner plates and serve immediately.

Courtesy of Owner Jomi Price and Chef Seth Foutz of Ketch 55 (p. 146)

Shrimp Salad

Driving up to Corolla may feel like you're driving to the end of the earth. But there's a heavenly stop before you get to the end of the road. North Banks Restaurant & Raw Bar, in the TimBuck II shopping center, has a fantastic menu featuring local, coastal cuisine, as well as great dishes from around the globe. I've enjoyed many lovely meals at this casual eatery.

Here's a great recipe for shrimp salad that can be used to fill lettuce leaves, or sandwich wraps, or in a bun, or enjoyed just by itself. It makes a vast quantity, perhaps good to have on hand for the start of a vacation. Otherwise, size it down according to your needs. If you have time, roast your own red peppers over a hot grill or under the broiler, then peel and chop.

Yield: About 12 servings

2 cups chopped celery

1 cup canned whole water chestnuts, rinsed and drained

1 cup chopped roasted red peppers

1 cup chopped red onion

6 pounds shrimp, cooked and chopped

2 to 3 cups mayonnaise, according to preference

1 teaspoon plus a pinch of cayenne pepper

1 teaspoon salt

1 teaspoon white pepper

Place the celery, water chestnuts, red pepper, and onion in the food processor. Process until all is finely minced. (Or finely chop all by hand.)

Transfer the mixture to a large bowl, and add other ingredients. Mix well. Chill and serve.

Courtesy of the North Banks Restaurant & Raw Bar (p. 42)

Simple Shrimp & Grits

Shrimp and grits show up on many Outer Banks menus. But it's not a traditional Outer Banks dish. Rather, it comes from the Low Country, further down the coast in South Carolina, where fishermen cooked up the smallest, less-marketable shrimp in reserved bacon grease and served them over grits for a filling breakfast. North Carolina can sort of claim the dish, as Bill Neal, chef and owner of Crook's Corner restaurant in Chapel Hill, NC, helped to put Shrimp and Grits on the nation's menus when a New York Times article featured his recipe in 1985.

But here's the irony of shrimp and grits on the Outer Banks. Prior to the 1930s, very few Bankers ate shrimp. They thought they were bugs, unfit for eating. They traded barrels of shrimp that fouled up their fishing nets for barrels of corn. The corn they dried, then took to one of the dozen windmills that dotted the Outer Banks, where it would be ground into cornmeal and grits. So, there is a historical connection between shrimp and grits!

You'll find some versions of shrimp and grits feature andouille or some other kind of spicy sausage. Low Country recipes use bacon, which I prefer too. Some Southerners cook their grits with a mixture of milk and heavy cream, or a blend of milk and water. My family is fairly lactose-intolerant, so we just use water, or better still, shrimp stock. And please be sure to use stone-ground grits, which have so much more texture and flavor.

I like to save shrimp shells in the freezer, and when shrimp stock is needed, simply simmer them with onions, celery, parsley, and a few peppercorns in water to cover. Drain, then use the stock in place of the water for cooking grits, which will give your finished grits a pinkish color.

Yield: 4 servings

For the Cheese Grits

4 cups water or shrimp stock

1 teaspoon salt

1 cup stone-ground grits, white or yellow

2 tablespoons butter

1 cup grated Parmigiano-Reggiano cheese

In a large heavy-bottom saucepan, bring the water and salt to a boil over medium high heat. Whisk in the grits, and turn the heat to very low. Cover. Cook, without stirring, for about 20 minutes, or until the water has almost disappeared.

Stir in the butter and cheese, and keep warm over very low heat or over a pot of hot water until serving time.

For the Shrimp

3 slices thick-cut bacon, cut into ½-inch pieces (use scissors for ease)

1 medium onion, finely chopped

2 tablespoons butter

2 pounds shrimp, shelled and deveined, then patted dry

1 teaspoon Old Bay, or to taste

2 tablespoons chopped chives

1 tablespoon minced garlic

2 tablespoons chopped fresh parsley

Salt and freshly ground pepper to taste

In a large sauté pan, place bacon pieces. Turn heat to medium, and cook until bacon is almost brown and fat is rendered (melted). Add onion, and cook for 3 to 5 minutes, until onion is tender and translucent.

Add butter to the pan, along with the shrimp. Sprinkle with the Old Bay and chives. Cook until the shrimp just turns pink. Quickly add the garlic and stir around. Sprinkle with parsley, then salt and pepper to taste. Remove the pan from the heat. Divide and serve over cooked cheese grits.

Courtesy of Elizabeth Wiegand

Herb-Onion Spoon Bread

The Blue Point in Duck is one of my very favorites. Long before it became trendy, chef and co-owner Sam McGann set out to serve a seasonal, coastal, and Southern menu that's always promoted local and sustainable seafood. The insistence on quality led to early accolades from critics and patrons alike, and continues today. We usually have to sneak a seat at the bar to avoid a long line if we overlooked making reservations. Or we just enjoy the gorgeous overlook of Currituck Sound and the setting sun while waiting for a table.

Spoon bread is an old, savory Southern treat found at sophisticated tables as well as in simple country kitchens. It's basically a baked pudding made with cornmeal. Chef McGann seasons his with lots of fresh herbs. You'll like serving this simple recipe as a side dish. Use a small, heavy cast-iron casserole with a lid, such as those made by Lodge or Le Creuset. And do try to find stone-ground cornmeal, for it has so much more flavor than the run-of-the-mill type.

Yield: About 6 servings

2 cups whole milk
1 cup heavy cream
4 tablespoons unsalted butter
1 dried or fresh bay leaf
¼ cup chopped chives
¾ cup white cornmeal

½ cup mixed chopped fresh herbs—parsley, tarragon, dill, mint, thyme
3 large eggs, slightly beaten
1 tablespoon salt (or less, to taste)
Freshly ground pepper, to taste

Preheat the oven to 350°F.

In a small, 2-quart cast-iron casserole at least 3 inches deep with lid (or any stovetop- and oven-safe casserole dish with lid), place the milk, cream, butter, bay leaf, and chives. Bring to a simmer over medium heat.

Whisk in the cornmeal and bring the mixture back to a simmer (small bubbles just beginning to form, especially on the outer edge of the pot). Reduce heat to very low and continue to stir, until the mixture begins to thicken.

Remove the bay leaf and fold in the mixed herbs. Quickly fold in the beaten eggs until evenly distributed. Season with salt and pepper, and cover.

Place the covered casserole dish in the preheated oven for 20 minutes, until custard is almost set. Remove cover and continue to bake for an additional 15 to 20 minutes until a nice crust has formed and the spoon bread is set in the middle. Cover and serve warm at the table.

Note: I only have a 6-quart casserole dish, so the spoon bread cooked much quicker, within a total of 20 to 25 minutes, and was not as thick or deep as typical spoon bread. But it was still totally awesome!

Courtesy of Sam McGann at The Blue Point (p. 53)

Sweet Potato Surprise

Amy Huggins Gaw, aka The Outer Banks Epicurean, has food on the brain, she says. As a personal chef, wedding caterer, or instructor for corporate training retreats, she preaches eating local and organically raised foods. She also developed Outer Banks SeaSalt, an all-natural salt derived from hand-processing seawater gathered near her home.

North Carolina is the nation's leading producer of sweet potatoes. With this recipe, Amy allows you to enjoy this veggie deliciously dolled up with a caramel sauce and salty, candied pecans, another local Southern treat. It's almost like a dessert. I love eating the pecans prepared this way as a sweet treat!

Don't be intimidated by the length of this recipe, or by having to make the caramel sauce. Amy's instructions make it easy. Note that it's best to have the salty candied pecans already made before starting on this recipe. And while the sweet potatoes are cooking you can make the caramel sauce.

Yield: 6 to 8 servings

For the Salty Candied Pecans

2½ cups pecans, preferably
  from NC, chopped

2 teaspoons butter, melted

1 cup sugar

1 teaspoon cinnamon

3 or 4 generous pinches of
  Outer Banks SeaSalt (or
  another sea salt)

¼ cup water

1 teaspoon vanilla

Preheat the oven to 300°F.

In a medium bowl, toss pecans in the butter. Spread on a lipped baking sheet, then roast in the oven for 20 to 25 minutes, stirring frequently, until pecans are toasted. Remove from oven and cool.

Combine the sugar, cinnamon, salt, and water in a large saucepan. Cook over medium heat, stirring until sugar is dissolved. Continue to cook until the mixture reaches 236 degrees, the soft-ball stage. Remove from heat, and add vanilla. Stir in the pecans until mixture is creamy.

Place a long sheet of waxed paper on a baking sheet or cutting board. Pour the pecans onto the waxed paper and use a fork to separate the pecans. Note they are very hot, so wait until they are cool to touch or pop one into your mouth. At this point you can sprinkle them with another pinch of Outer Banks SeaSalt if preferred. Store in a closed container if needed.

For the Cooked Sweet Potatoes

6 large organic sweet potatoes　　**3 tablespoons butter**
Pinch of Outer Banks SeaSalt

Peel and cube the sweet potatoes. Place in a saucepan, and fill the pan with just enough water to cover the potatoes. Over medium heat, bring to a simmer and cook until potatoes are soft. Remove from heat, drain, and return to the stovetop. Over very low heat, using a potato masher, mash potatoes with butter and another pinch of Outer Banks SeaSalt.

For the Caramel Sauce

1 cup sugar　　**½ cup heavy cream**
6 tablespoons butter, cut into
**　1-inch slices**

Have everything ready before you put the pan on the stove, as this recipe progresses quickly.

Place the sugar in a 3-quart saucepan and heat over moderately high heat. As the sugar begins to melt, stir constantly.

As soon as the sugar comes to a boil, stop stirring. The mixture will begin to darken in color, and when it's dark amber and all of the sugar crystals have melted, immediately add the butter to the pan. (When you add the butter and the cream, the mixture will foam up considerably.) Whisk constantly until the butter has melted.

Then take the pan off the heat. Wait a few seconds, then slowly add the cream to the pan and continue to whisk to incorporate. (It will foam up again.) Whisk until the caramel sauce is smooth.

The caramel sauce may be drizzled over the cooked sweet potatoes at this point. If not using immediately, cool, then pour into a glass container and store in the refrigerator for up to two weeks.

To Assemble the Dish

You may prepare individual servings of sweet potato, or if you prefer, place all the sweet potatoes in a serving bowl. In either case, drizzle the caramel sauce over the cooked, hot sweet potatoes. Drop the salty candied pecans over the surface.

Courtesy of Amy Huggins Gaw, aka The Outer Banks Epicurean (p. 29 & p. 61)

Appendices

Appendix A: Eateries by Cuisine

American

Aqua (Duck), 52

Back Porch Restaurant & Wine Bar (Ocracoke), 167

Basnight's Lone Cedar Cafe (Nags Head), 102

Billfish Bar & Grill (Hatteras Village), 156

Blue Moon Beach Grill (Nags Head), 103

Breakwater Restaurant (Hatteras Village), 157

Cafe Atlantic (Ocracoke), 167

Cafe Pamlico (Buxton), 139

Cravings (Duck), 54

Creekside Cafe (Ocracoke), 169

Dajio's (Ocracoke), 170

Darrell's (Manteo), 124

Dinky's (Hatteras Village), 158

Elizabeth's Cafe (Duck), 55

1587 Restaurant (Manteo), 124

Fin & Claw Sea Grill, The (Corolla), 38

Fishbone's Sunset Grille & Raw Bar (Duck), 56

Flying Melon (Ocracoke), 171

Full Moon Cafe & Brewery (Manteo), 126

Jason's Restaurant (Ocracoke), 173

JK's Steaks & Seafood (Corolla), 39

Kelly's Outer Banks Restaurant & Tavern (Nags Head), 107

Ketch 55 Seafood Grill (Avon), 146

Kill Devil Grill, The (Kill Devil Hills), 81

Kimball's Kitchen (Duck), 56

Burgers

Tortugas' Lie (Nags Head), 116

Cal-Mex
See Mexican, 216

Caribbean
Goombays Grill & Raw Bar (Kill Devil Hills), 76
Rusty's (Buxton), 149

Coffeehouse
Coffeehouse on Roanoke Island, The (Manteo), 131
Dancing Turtle Coffee Shop (Hatteras Village), 161
Duck Cottage (Duck), 64
Duck Donuts (Duck), 55
Front Porch Cafe, The (Kill Devil Hills), 97
Front Porch Cafe, The (Manteo), 132
Front Porch Cafe, The (Nags Head), 119
Live Oak Coffee (Ocracoke), 179
Morning View Coffee House (Nags Head), 120
Ocracoke Coffee Company (Ocracoke), 179

Outer Banks Coffee Company (Corolla), 49
Southern Bean (Kitty Hawk), 98
Shack Coffee Shop & Beer Garden, The (Corolla), 49
Tullio's Pastry Shop (Duck), 63
Waverider's Coffee & Deli (Nags Head), 120

Deli
Cafe Lachine (Nags Head), 106
Good Life Eatery, The (Kitty Hawk), 75
Great Gut Deli (Wanchese), 126
Harbor Deli (Hatteras Village), 159
Lighthouse Bagels Donuts & Deli (Corolla), 39
Lovie's Kitchen Table (Corolla), 39
Miss Helen's Stop Quick (Nags Head), 110
Poor Richard's Sandwich Shop (Manteo), 129
Stop N Shop (Kill Devil Hills), 90
Waves Market & Deli (Waves), 151

Pan-American

Rundown Cafe & Tsunami Bar
(Kitty Hawk), 88

Pasta/Pizza

American Pie Pizza & Homemade
Ice Cream (Kill Devil Hills), 92
Angelo's Pizza (Buxton), 152
Bambino's Little Italy (Corolla), 44
Beach Road Pizza (Corolla), 44
Cafe 12 (Avon), 140
Cafe Franco's (Kill Devil Hills), 92
Colington Pizza (Kill Devil
Hills), 92
Corolla Pizza & Deli (Corolla), 45
Cosmo's Pizza (Corolla), 45
Dare Devil Pizzeria (Kill Devil
Hills), 92
Duck Pizza Company (Duck), 59
Giant Slice Pizza (Corolla), 45
Gidget's Pizza and Pasta
(Avon), 152
Gingerbread House, The
(Frisco), 152
Island Garden Deli & Pizzeria
(Manteo), 129
La Dolce Vita (Corolla), 45

Lisa's Pizzeria (Rodanthe), 152
Max's Pizza Company (Kitty
Hawk), 92
Nino's Pizza (Avon), 152
Papa Nino's (Buxton), 153
Pasquale's Pizza & Pub
(Corolla), 45
Pizza Stop (Southern Shores), 93
Pizzazz Pizza (Corolla), 46
Pizzazz Pizza (Duck), 59
Rocco's Pizza (Hatteras
Village), 160
Slice Pizzeria (Kill Devil Hills), 93
Tomato Patch Pizzeria
(Corolla), 46
Wave Pizza Cafe, The (Duck), 60

Seafood

Aqua (Duck), 52
Atlantic Coast Cafe (Waves &
Avon), 138
Awful Arthur's (Kill Devil Hills), 70
Back Porch Restaurant & Wine Bar
(Ocracoke), 167
Barefoot Bernie's (Kitty Hawk), 71
Basnight's Lone Cedar Cafe (Nags
Head), 102

Dockside North Seafood Market (Corolla), 48

Green Acre Market (Duck), 62

Harbor House Seafood Market (Hatteras Village), 160

I Got Your Crabs Seafood Market & Steam Bar (Kitty Hawk), 95

Island Spice & Wine (Avon), 154

La Isla Mexican Grocery (Ocracoke), 177

La Mexicana Mini Mart (Kill Devil Hills), 95

Lee Robinson General Store (Hatteras Village), 160

Manteo Farmers Market (Manteo), 130

Nags Head Produce (Nags Head), 118

O'Neals Sea Harvest Market & Cafe (Manteo), 131

Ocracoke Seafood Market (Ocracoke), 177

Ocracoke Variety Store (Ocracoke), 178

Risky Business Seafood (Avon), 154

Risky Business Seafood (Hatteras Village), 161

St. Waves Seafood & Produce (Waves), 155

Seaside Farm Market (Corolla), 48

Seaside Gourmet To Go (Kitty Hawk), 96

Shrimp On The Go (Kill Devil Hills), 96

Steamer's Shellfish To Go (Corolla), 48

Sticky Bottom Produce (Hatteras Village), 161

Surf's Up Seafood Market (Avon), 155

Sweet T's (Duck), 62

Tarheel Too (Kill Devil Hills), 97

Tommy's Gourmet Market & Wine Emporium (Duck), 63

Trio: Wine Beer Cheese (Kitty Hawk), 97

Tullio's Pastry Shop (Duck), 63

Whalebone Seafood Market (Nags Head), 119

Zillie's Pantry (Ocracoke), 178

Steak

JK's Steaks & Seafood (Corolla), 39

Appendix B:
Craft Brews &
Local Wineries

Breweries

The Outer Banks boast several microbrews, hand-crafted and tasty. And what more you do need than an ice-cold, local brew on a hot summer's day? Visit these breweries for a taste or a tour.

The Full Moon Brewery, 208 Queen Elizabeth St., Manteo; (252) 473-6666; thefullmooncafe.com. Located on a corner near the waterfront in Manteo, this small brewery specializes in British- and Irish-style beers, using a malt as the base, then adding more malt flavors or roasted barley. The tiny brew house is just a one-barrel RIMS system filling either one or two barrel fermenters. I like the Lost Colony Ale, with its sweet, malty taste, plus flavors of caramel, coffee, and molasses. A more citrusy ale with a peppery hop finish is the Baltimore Blonde. They also do a rather robust dry Irish stout. Tours and tastings are available. Enjoy an informal meal on the sidewalk, or a full menu inside the cafe.

Outer Banks Brewing Station, 600 S. Croatan Hwy., MP 8.5, Kill Devil Hills; (252) 449-2739; obbrewing.com. Outer Banks Brewing Station, built to look like an old Outer Banks life-saving station, was the country's very first wind-powered brewery, and prides itself on being innovative and environmentally "green." Brews are done seasonally, although their Olsch, brewed in the Kolsch style, is available all the time. I like the refreshing summertime lemongrass wheat ale, a World Beer Cup Silver Medal winner. The golden rose ale is made with hops, then cool fermented with an ale yeast, and the American-styled IPA has a sweet malty flavor. There's also a very rich porter they call "Poobah." Two-liter to-go growlers can be purchased and brought back for refilling in their bottle. A full food menu is served, along with live music some nights.

Weeping Radish Farm Brewery, 6810 Caratoke Hwy., Grandy; (252) 491-5205; weepingradish.com. This bustling enterprise moved from its Manteo location, up the beach and over the northern bridge to Grandy on Route 158. There, owner Uli Bennewitz established an eco farm, where award-winning specialty meats are made by a butcher-in-residence from Germany and sold to area gourmet markets and served at the Pub on the property. As the oldest microbrewery in North Carolina, the Weeping Radish has had a long struggle here until the legislature passed a bill that would allow beer to be sold on-site. Now, they continue to expand their list of all natural brews. Uli, the owner, was raised in Bavaria, and was determined to make a quality brew using the strict *Reinheitsgebot* Purity Law of 1516. The Corolla Gold, a medium-bodied sweet malt, the OBX Kolsch, with a more delicate, fruity flavor, and the IPA 25, made with fresh NC hops, are on the lighter side. The Fest has a bit of hop bitterness, brewed in the Marzen style, and the Black Radish is a dark German lager. I'm loving the Hefeweizen, a traditional light-bodied wheat beer. If you can't make it out to the pub or brewery, or find it in your local market, beer may be ordered online, as long as you and the person receiving the beer are at least 21 years of age.

Wineries

Martin Vineyards, 213 Martin Farm Ln., Knotts Island; (252) 429-3542; martin vineyards.com. After successfully growing peaches and Scuppernong grapes, the Martin family planted some vinifera grape varieties in this rich coastal soil. They now produce a Chardonnay and a Meritage, and  a couple of blends of Muscadines, along with a peach wine hand-crafted with peaches from their orchard.

Sanctuary Vineyards, the Cotton Gin, 6957 Caratoke Hwy., Jarvis-burg; (252) 491-2387; sanctuaryvineyards.com. With seven genera-tions of farming behind them, the Wright family has about 10 acres of grapevines nestled between rows of corn and nesting migratory snow geese. Like most vines grown in the South, they struggle with intense heat, but here they've got cooling breezes from the Atlantic and ancient sand dunes with great drainage. Norton, a good grape for the South, and Sangiovese are grown along with two French hybrids, as well as the great Muscadine grapes that were growing here when the first European settlers rowed by. Bottles include the Wild Pony White, and a Chardonnay and Viognier. The vineyard's tasting room is in the historic Cotton Gin in Jarvisburg, where they hold an annual food and wine festival every September. An oyster roast, The Big Curri-Shuck, is held at the vineyard around Thanksgiving. Both feature live music and wine tastings.

Appendix C: Personal Chef Services

When you're on vacation, especially at the beach, sometimes the last thing you want to do is shake off all the sand and head into the kitchen to cook a meal for a hungry crowd. And when it's high season, you can bet on a wait at any restaurant on the Outer Banks. You've got the take-out option, or steamer pots, but take it up a notch and treat your family and friends—and yourself—to a personal chef who will come in to your kitchen, and prepare a meal you've discussed and ordered, and then (the best part to me) cleans up!

Cafe 111 Personal Chef Service, (252) 256-2433; cafe111obx .com. Chef Jamie Pauls brings three to five courses you select from appetizers and salads, like mini crab cakes or caprese stacks, with entrees made from fresh seafood, like barely seared tuna, or shrimp and grits, or filet mignon finished in an iron skillet. Desserts are too tempting . . . peanut butter cheesecake or blueberry pie with homemade ice cream.

Chefs On Call—Red Sky Cafe, (252) 261-8646; partycateringobx
.com. Chef Wes Stepp from the Red Sky Cafe in Duck will help you
coordinate a "culinary adventure" with one of his professional chefs
at your place. Multiple courses, from appetizers to desserts, can be
selected from a menu that reflects the Cafe's Southwestern take on
fresh local seafood, or the menu can be tailored to your own wishes.

Outer Banks Epicurean, outerbanksepicurean.com. Amy Huggins
Gaw is the creator and energetic force of Outer Banks Epicurean, Inc.,
what she calls a "culinary adventure business"—like paddling kayaks
around Colington Island, visiting crab shedders, and then going back
to the kitchen to cook those soft shells. She offers cooking lessons,
corporate training retreats, and personal chef services, where
she'll come cook in your home or rental, or cater an event. She's
also joined forces with Outer Banks Wedding & Etiquette Library.
Reach her via her website listed above. Outer Banks Epicurean also
provides precooked meals, with each dish individually packaged
and refrigerated, so that you heat and eat on your own schedule.
It's slow food for busy people, says Amy, who gathers her organic,
locally grown ingredients from Beach Organics in
Grandy, where you order on Wednesday and
make your pickup (or there is
a limited delivery, too) on
Friday (call Beach Organics
at 252-457-0200). And, she
and husband John Gaw are the
creators of Outer Banks SeaSalt,

a marvelous white, flaky salt made by gathering buckets of water from the ocean and then working her kitchen magic. You can find that product on her website or at several of the specialty markets on the Outer Banks. See Amy's recipes for **Oysters Rock-Yer-Fella** (p. 195) and **Sweet Potato Surprise** (p. 207).

Outer Banks Personal Chef, (252) 480-2332; outerbanks personalchef.com. Chef Lynn Flowers will provide private gigs in your home or cottage, and will also cater large parties. After a decade of cooking here, she knows the regional cuisine and will help select a menu that works for everyone in your group. With a background of cooking Italian style, she can do hand-rolled pasta and sear sea scallops or NC shrimp. Brownie cake with peanut caramel sauce, tiramisu, or an ice cream pie are tempting finales.

Index

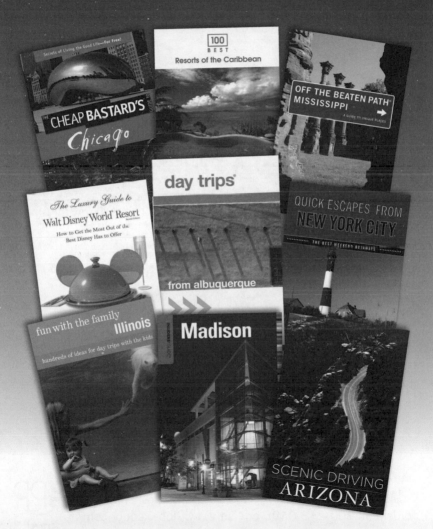

Getaway ideas for the local traveler

Need a day away to relax, refresh, renew?
Just get in your car and go!